AN INTRODUCTION
TO THE
PARABLES OF JESUS

Books by Robert H. Stein
Published by The Westminster Press

An Introduction to the Parables of Jesus

The Method and Message of Jesus' Teachings

AN INTRODUCTION
TO THE
PARABLES OF JESUS

BY
ROBERT H. STEIN

THE WESTMINSTER PRESS
PHILADELPHIA

BOOK DESIGN BY ALICE DERR

First edition

Published by The Westminster Press®
Philadelphia, Pennyslvania

PRINTED IN THE UNITED STATES OF AMERICA
9 8 7 6 5 4 3 2 1

Library of Congress Cataloging in Publication Data

Stein, Robert H., 1935–
  An introduction to the parables of Jesus.

  Includes bibliographical references and indexes.
  1. Jesus Christ—Parables. I. Title.
BT377.S75   226'.806   81-11564
ISBN 0-664-24390-8   AACR2

TO
JULIE, KEITH, AND STEPHEN

For this child I prayed; and the LORD has
granted me my petition which I made to him.
Therefore I have lent him to the LORD;
as long as he lives, he is lent to the LORD.
                                    1 Samuel 1:27-28

CONTENTS

ABBREVIATIONS

b. Shab.	The tractate "Shabbath" in the Babylonian Talmud
BJRL	*Bulletin of the John Rylands University Library of Manchester*
CBQ	*The Catholic Biblical Quarterly*
CSEL	*Corpus Scriptorum Ecclesiasticorum Latinorum*
ET	*The Expository Times*
GT	Gospel of Thomas
JBL	*Journal of Biblical Literature*
JJS	*Journal of Jewish Studies*
JTS	*Journal of Theological Studies*
L	Material unique to the Gospel of Luke
Loeb	The Loeb Classical Library
LUKE	Material in the Gospel of Luke that is also found in the Gospel of Matthew, i.e., the Q material in Luke
Luke	Material that is found only in the Gospel of Luke, i.e., the L material
LXX	The Greek translation of the Old Testament, called the Septuagint
M	Material unique to the Gospel of Matthew
MARK	Material in the Gospel of Mark that is also found in either the Gospel of Matthew, the Gospel of Luke, or both
Mark	Material that is found only in the Gospel of Mark
MATT	Material in the Gospel of Matthew that is also found in the Gospel of Luke, i.e., the Q material in Matthew
Matt	Material that is found only in the Gospel of Matthew, i.e., the M material
NPNF	*Nicene and Post-Nicene Fathers*
NT	*Novum Testamentum*

NTS   *New Testament Studies*
PL   *Patrologia Latina*
Q   A hypothetical source used by Matthew and Luke in
           writing their Gospels, i.e., the material common to
           Matthew and Luke but not found in Mark
SJT   *Scottish Journal of Theology*
TDNT   *Theological Dictionary of the New Testament*
ZNW   *Zeitschrift für die Neutestamentliche Wissenschaft*
ZTK   *Zeitschrift für Theologie und Kirche*

PREFACE

THE IDEA FOR THIS PRESENT WORK arose out of my teaching a
number of classes dealing with the parables of Jesus. In seeking texts
for these classes, I found none that truly suited my own purposes and
aims. As a result I have sought to provide an introduction to the
parables that would meet that need. I have followed somewhat the
basic pattern set forth in Chapter 3 of *The Method and Message of Jesus'
Teachings*. I have, of course, gone into much greater detail in this regard
and have added four chapters which deal with the content of Jesus'
parables.

The work, itself, consists of ten chapters which can be divided into
two main sections. The first deals in general with the issue of how to
interpret the parables. I cover such questions as what a parable is
(Chapter 1); why Jesus taught in parables (Chapter 2); where the
parables came from (Chapter 3); how to interpret the parables
(Chapters 4 and 5); and give an example of how to interpret the
parables (Chapter 6). The second main division deals with the praxis of
interpretation. Here I deal at length with a specific parable which
teaches a major theme of Jesus and briefly with one or more additional
parables in which the same theme is taught. The subjects are the
kingdom of God as a present reality (Chapter 7); the demand of the
parables; i.e., the call to decision (Chapter 8); the God of the parables
(Chapter 9); and the final judgment (Chapter 10).

I have again used in the present work the designations MARK,
Mark, MATT, Matt, LUKE, and Luke which I used in *The Method and
Message of Jesus' Teachings*. This method of designating the Markan, Q,
M, and L material was well received in the original work, so that I
thought it profitable to continue it here. The reader is referred to the list

of Abbreviations for a description of what is meant by these designations. Again it should be pointed out that it is not always certain as to whether a passage should be designated as MARK, Q, L, or M, but in the vast majority of instances these designations are quite helpful in revealing at a glance the nature of the material being discussed.

I would like to thank a number of persons for their help in preparing this work for publication. Unfortunately I cannot mention all of them, but I would like especially to single out William Healy and Eric Tanquist, who have interacted at great length with me on each chapter of the work. I would also like to thank the faculty secretary, Lori Jass, for her diligence and care in typing the final manuscript. Finally I would like to thank my wife, Joan, and my children, Julie, Keith, and Stephen, for their patience and understanding during the writing of this work.

All biblical quotations in this work come from the Revised Standard Version of the Bible unless otherwise specified.

R. H. S.

CHAPTER 1

WHAT IS A PARABLE?

OF ALL THE FORMS that Jesus used in his teaching, by far the most familiar and striking is the parable. The familiarity of Jesus' parables and their pervasiveness is evident in that both Christian and non-Christian alike speak of "burying one's talent" (Matt 25:25), "counting the cost" (Luke 14:28), being a "good Samaritan" (Luke 10:29-37), etc., frequently without realizing that in so doing they are in fact quoting from the parables of Jesus. The amount of parabolic material contained in our Gospels is quite impressive, for it is estimated that over one third of the teachings of Jesus found in the first three Gospels is found in parables.

Yet what is a parable? In church school, children are taught that a parable is "an earthly story with a heavenly meaning." This, as we shall see, is only partly true. If we look for a definition of the term in an English dictionary or encyclopedia, we shall find that a parable is usually defined as: "a short allegorical story, designed to convey some truth or moral lesson" or "a brief story using events or facts of everyday life to illustrate a moral or spiritual truth." In general, it would appear that the standard dictionary meaning of the term "parable" defines it as a story of everyday happenings which is meant to convey some moral or spiritual principle. The problem with this approach, however, is that a modern dictionary or encyclopedia tells us primarily what the English word "parable" means to twentieth-century English-speaking people. Yet the New Testament was not written in twentieth-century English for twentieth-century readers whose native tongue is English!

The New Testament was, of course, written in Greek, and the term that we find in our Gospels is the Greek term *parabolē*. It would therefore appear wiser to look up in a Greek dictionary what this term meant to first-century Greek-speaking people in order to understand what a parable is in the Gospels. When we do this, we discover that a *parabolē* is an illustration, a comparison, or an analogy, usually in story form, using common events of everyday life to reveal a moral or a spiritual truth. Again, however, we encounter a problem, for a classical or koine Greek dictionary will tell us what the term *parabolē* meant in the Greek-speaking world of classical or New Testament times, *but* Jesus did not live in a primarily Greek-speaking environment! While it is probable that Jesus could understand and speak Greek (note MARK 7:24-30, 31f.; 15:2f.), his native tongue was Aramaic. This is clearly demonstrated by the Aramaic terms still present in our Gospels which come from his lips (note MARK 9:47; 15:34; Mark 3:17; 5:41; 14:36; MATT 6:24; 12:27; 13:33; Matt 5:22; 10:25; 16:17; John 1:42; etc.).[1] As a result, a classical or even a koine Greek dictionary will not define for us what a "parable" signified for Jesus.

In seeking to understand what Jesus meant by the term "parable," we need to understand what the term that the New Testament translates *parabolē* meant. The Hebrew/Aramaic term that Jesus used in his conversation was the term *mashal*. We know this because when the Hebrew Old Testament was translated into Greek in the second and third centuries before Christ, the term *mashal* was translated by the Greek word *parabolē*. In fact, in this translation, called the Septuagint, or LXX, in every instance except two (Eccl 1:17; Sirach 47:11) the term *parabolē* was used to translate the term *mashal*. Since, therefore, Jesus spoke in *mashalim* rather than *parabolai*, it is important to understand what a *mashal* meant in the Old Testament in our search to understand just what Jesus meant by the term *mashal*→*parabolē*→parable.

"Parable" in the Old Testament

In the Old Testament a *mashal* refers to far more than simply an "earthly story with a heavenly meaning." At times it can refer to a simple PROVERB.

> What do you mean by repeating this proverb [*mashal*] concerning the land of Israel, "The fathers have eaten sour grapes, and the children's teeth are set on edge"? (Ezek 18:2-3)
>
> As the proverb [*mashal*] of the ancients says, "Out of the wicked comes forth wickedness. . . ." (1 Sam 24:13)[2]

Other examples of how the term *mashal* is used to describe a proverb can be found in 1 Sam 10:12; Ezek 12:22-23; 16:44.

A *mashal* can also refer to a BYWORD, SATIRE, TAUNT, or WORD OF DERISION.

> When the LORD has given you rest . . . , you will take up
> this taunt [*mashal*] against the king of Babylon:
>   "How the oppressor has ceased,
>   the insolent fury ceased!" (Isa 14:3-4)

> Shall not all these take up their taunt [*mashal*] against him, in
> scoffing derision of him, and say,
>   "Woe to him who heaps up what is not his own—
>   for how long?—
>   and loads himself with pledges!" (Hab 2:6)

Other examples of this use of the term can be found in Num 21:27-30;[3] Deut 28:37; 1 Kings 9:7; 2 Chron 7:20;[4] and Ps 44:14;[5] 69:11.[6]

Another way in which the term *mashal* is used in the Old Testament is with reference to RIDDLES.

> I will open my mouth in a parable [*mashal*];
>   I will utter dark sayings from of old. (Ps 78:2)[7]

> Son of man, propound a riddle, and speak an allegory [*mashal*] to
> the house of Israel; say, Thus says the Lord GOD: A great eagle with
> great wings and long pinions. . . . (Ezek 17:2f.)

Two other instances in which *mashal* refers to a riddle are Ps 49:4[8] and Prov 1:6.[9]

A final use of this term in the Old Testament is to describe a STORY or an ALLEGORY.

> Son of man, write down the name of this day, this very day. The
> king of Babylon has laid siege to Jerusalem this very day. And utter
> an allegory [*mashal*] to the rebellious house and say to them, Thus
> says the Lord GOD:
>   Set on the pot, set it on,
>   pour in water also;
>   put in it the pieces of flesh,
>   all the good pieces, the thigh and the shoulder;
>   fill it with choice bones.
>   Take the choicest one of the flock,
>   pile the logs under it;
>   boil its pieces,
>   seethe also its bones in it. (Ezek 24:2-5)

Two other examples where a *mashal* refers to a story parable or an allegory are Ezek 17:2-10 and 20:49 to 21:5.[10] There exist three other examples in the Old Testament of this kind of *mashal* where the term itself is not used. Despite the absence of the term in these instances, however, it is quite clear that they are examples of *mashalim*. The most famous of these is the well-known parable of Nathan in 2 Sam 12:1-4. The two others are 2 Sam 14:1-11 and Isa 5:1-7.

It is clearly evident from the above that a parable in the Old Testament included a much wider variety of concepts than simply stories that contained moral or spiritual truths. Frequently a parable is not a story at all!

"PARABLE" IN THE NEW TESTAMENT

It is not surprising that in the New Testament the term *parabolē* also refers to a broad spectrum of similar concepts. As in the Old Testament, it can refer to a PROVERB.

> And he said to them, "Doubtless you will quote to me this proverb [*parabolē*], 'Physician, heal yourself. . . .' " (Luke 4:23)

> He also told them a parable: "Can a blind man lead a blind man? Will they not both fall into a pit?" (LUKE 6:39. The parallel in MATT 15:14 lacks the term *parabolē*; cf. MARK 3:23-24 for another example)

A *parabolē* can also refer to a METAPHOR or FIGURATIVE SAYING.

> And he called the people to him again, and said to them, "Hear me, all of you, and understand: there is nothing outside a man which by going into him can defile him; but the things which come out of a man are what defile him." And when he had entered the house, and left the people, his disciples asked him about the parable. (MARK 7:14-17)

> He told them a parable also: "No one tears a piece from a new garment and puts it upon an old garment; if he does, he will tear the new, and the piece from the new will not match the old. And no one puts new wine into old wineskins; if he does, the new wine will burst the skins and it will be spilled, and the skins will be destroyed. But new wine must be put into fresh wineskins." (LUKE 5:36-38. The parallels in MARK 2:21-22 and MATT 9:16-17 lack the term *parabolē*.)

There are a number of ways of making a comparison. A metaphor is one. A simile is another. The difference between the two is that whereas a metaphor makes an implicit comparison between two unlike things, a simile makes an explicit comparison by means of such terms as "like," "as," "as if," "seems." The most famous definition of these two terms is undoubtedly that of Aristotle, who states in his work *Rhetoric* 2, 20, 2ff.:

> The simile also is a metaphor; for there is very little difference. When the poet says of Achilles, "he rushed on like a lion," it is a simile; if he says, "A lion, he rushed on," it is a metaphor; for because both are courageous, he transfers the sense and calls Achilles a lion. (Loeb)[11]

When a simile is expanded from a simple explicit comparison into a picture, we then have a SIMILITUDE. Generally a similitude involves a comparing of something like the kingdom of God to a typical occurrence of daily life.

> And he said, "With what can we compare the kingdom of God, or what parable shall we use for it? It is like a grain of mustard seed, which, when sown upon the ground, is the smallest of all the seeds on earth; yet when it is sown it grows up and becomes the greatest of all shrubs, and puts forth large branches, so that the birds of the air can make nests in its shade." (MARK 4:30-32)

> He told them another parable. "The kingdom of heaven is like leaven which a woman took and hid in three measures of flour, till it was all leavened." (MATT 13:33)

Other examples can be found in Mark 4:26-29; MARK 13:28-29; MATT 7:9-11; LUKE 15:4-7; Luke 15:8-10; 17:7-10.

When a similitude is expanded from a picture into a story, we then have either a story parable, an example parable, or an "allegory." A story parable refers to a singular event. Unlike a similitude, which begins with a general statement of a daily occurrence ("What man of you," Luke 15:4; "Which of you," Luke 11:5; "What father among you," LUKE 11:11; etc.), a STORY PARABLE refers to a singular incident ("There was a rich man," Luke 16:1; "A man had two sons," Matt 21:28; "A man once gave a great banquet," LUKE 14:16; etc.). The following is a good example of a STORY PARABLE:

> But he said to him, "A man once gave a great banquet, and invited many; and at the time for the banquet he sent his servant to say to those who had been invited, 'Come; for all is now ready.' But they all alike began to make excuses. The first said to him, 'I have bought a field, and I must go out and see it; I pray you, have me excused.' And another said, 'I have bought five yoke of oxen, and I go to examine them; I pray you, have me excused.' And another

said, 'I have married a wife, and therefore I cannot come.' So the
servant came and reported this to his master. Then the
householder in anger said to his servant, 'Go out quickly to the
streets and lanes of the city, and bring in the poor and maimed and
blind and lame.' And the servant said, 'Sir, what you commanded
has been done, and still there is room.' And the master said to the
servant, 'Go out to the highways and hedges, and compel people
to come in, that my house may be filled. For I tell you, none of
those men who were invited shall taste my banquet.' " (LUKE
14:16-24)

Additional examples of story parables can be found in Matt 21:28-31;
25:1-13; MATT 25:14-30; Luke 15:11-32; 16:1-8; 18:2-8.

Closely related to story parables are EXAMPLE PARABLES. It is primarily
these two types of parables which come to mind when we think of the
parables of Jesus. The separation of these parables into two categories
is somewhat arbitrary, but the main difference appears to be that,
whereas a story parable provides an analogy between "an earthly story
and a heavenly truth," an example parable can end with a "Go and do
likewise" (Luke 10:37) or its negative equivalent. As a result, the
meaning of an example parable tends to lie closer to the "surface" of
the parable than in the case of a story parable, since the former serves
primarily as a model for behavior. Another way of saying this is that in
an example parable the "picture part" and the "reality part," i.e., what
the picture or metaphor is seeking to say, correspond more closely.[12]
The following is a well-known EXAMPLE PARABLE:

And he told them a parable, saying, "The land of a rich man
brought forth plentifully; and he thought to himself, 'What shall I
do, for I have nowhere to store my crops?' And he said, 'I will do
this: I will pull down my barns, and build larger ones; and there I
will store all my grain and my goods. And I will say to my soul,
Soul, you have ample goods laid up for many years; take your
ease, eat, drink, be merry.' But God said to him, 'Fool! This night
your soul is required of you; and the things you have prepared,
whose will they be?' So is he who lays up treasure for himself, and
is not rich toward God." (Luke 12:16-21)

Other examples can be found in Matt 18:23-25; Luke 10:29-37; 14:7-14;
16:19-31; 18:9-14.

In contrast to a story parable or an example parable, which are single
extended metaphors, an allegory has traditionally been understood as
a story that contains a string of metaphors. As a result, whereas a story
or an example parable has one main point of comparison, an allegory

has several.[13] Undoubtedly the most famous allegory in the English language is John Bunyan's *The Pilgrim's Progress.* In this allegory the names of various characters as well as the names of various places are in no way incidental. On the contrary, it is important to note that the names of the various characters (Christian, Worldly Wiseman, Evangelist, Malice, Love-lust, Hate-light, Legality, Piety, Charity, Money-love, Faithful, etc.), as well as the various places (Destruction, Salvation, Vanity Fair, Zion, Gulf of Despond, River of Water of Life, etc.), are of primary importance for interpreting the allegory. To disregard these names and what they signify would be to miss much of the story, for in an allegory these details are not simply local coloring or fill-in material but vital components of the story which must be noted and interpreted.

There has been a great deal of debate over whether any of the parables of Jesus are allegorical in nature. This issue of whether Jesus himself ever used allegory shall be discussed later.[14] At this point, however, it need only be pointed out that in its present form in the Gospels, MARK 12:1-11 is allegorical in nature and must therefore be classified as an ALLEGORY.

> And he began to speak to them in parables. "A man planted a vineyard, and set a hedge around it, and dug a pit for the wine press, and built a tower, and let it out to tenants, and went into another country. When the time came, he sent a servant to the tenants, to get from them some of the fruit of the vineyard. And they took him and beat him, and sent him away empty-handed. Again he sent to them another servant, and they wounded him in the head, and treated him shamefully. And he sent another, and him they killed; and so with many others, some they beat and some they killed. He had still one other, a beloved son; finally he sent him to them, saying, 'They will respect my son.' But those tenants said to one another, 'This is the heir; come, let us kill him, and the inheritance will be ours.' And they took him and killed him, and cast him out of the vineyard. What will the owner of the vineyard do? He will come and destroy the tenants, and give the vineyard to others. Have you not read this scripture:
> 'The very stone which the builders rejected
> has become the head of the corner;
> this was the Lord's doing,
> and it is marvelous in our eyes'?" (MARK 12:1-11)

Other examples of allegory in the Gospels are Matt 13:24-29 and 36-43; MATT 22:1-14; MARK 4:3-9 and 13-20.[15]

THE NUMBER OF PARABLES IN THE GOSPELS

From the discussion above it is clear that a parable is more than "an earthly story with a heavenly meaning." At times in the Old Testament and/or the New Testament a parable (*mashal* or *parabolē*) can refer to a proverb, a simile (whether extended into a similitude or not), a taunt, a riddle, or a metaphor, as well as to various kinds of story type of parables and allegories. As a result, defining what a parable is becomes most difficult. Some scholars have even stated that any such attempt is hopeless because of the variety of figures the term describes.[16] It might be more convenient if we would limit the term "parable" to story and example parables, for this corresponds more closely with what people today mean by the term, but neither the Old Testament *mashal* nor the New Testament *parabolē* can be defined so narrowly, and we should not force the Scriptures to accept our definition of a parable, but on the contrary we should seek to understand how the Scriptures define this term. On the other hand, it might be more reasonable to consider every simile, metaphor, and proverb, as well as every similitude, story and example parable, and allegory parable. This would appear, however, to be too inclusive. Simply for convenience we shall define a parable as a figure of speech in which there is a brief or extended comparison.[17] This will not encompass all the figures which the terms *mashal* and *parabolē* designate, but it will cover the majority of them. We should, furthermore, keep in mind that the biblical use of the term does not permit any exact definition and that our definition is at best a general definition for the sake of convenience.

When we define a parable in this broad manner,[18] it then becomes impossible to list the exact number of parables contained in the Gospels. We shall nevertheless attempt to list them according to the degree of certainty that they are in fact parables.

Parables in Which the Term "Parable" Is Used as a Designation[19]

Mark 2:21 // Matt 9:16 // Luke 5:36 // cf. GT 47[20]	Patch
Mark 3:23-26 // Matt 12:25-26 // Luke 11:17-18	Divided house
Mark 4:2-9, *13-20* // Matt 13:3-9, *18-23* // Luke 8:4-8, *11-15* // cf. GT 9	Soils/Sower
Mark 4:21-22 // Luke 8:16-17 (included because of Mark 4:34)	Light under a bushel
Mark 4:24-25 // Luke 8:18 (included because of Mark 4:34)	Measure for measure
Mark 4:*26*-29 (included because of Mark 4:34)	Seed growing secretly

Mark 4:30-32 // Matt 13:31-32 // Luke 13:18-19 //   Mustard seed
  cf. GT 20

Mark 7:14-15 // Matt 15:10-11 (Note Mark 7:17 //   What defiles
  Matt 15:15)

Mark 12:1-11 // Matt 21:33-43 // Luke 20:9-17 //   Evil tenants
  cf. GT 65

Mark 13:28-29 // Matt 24:32-33 // Luke 21:29-31   Fig tree

Matt 13:24-30, 36-43 // cf. GT 57   Wheat and tares
Matt 13:33 // Luke 13:20-21 // cf. GT 96   Leaven
Matt 13:44 (included because of Matt 13:34-35,   Hidden treasure
  53) // cf. GT 109
Matt 13:45 46 (included because of Matt   Pearl
  13:34-35, 53) // cf. GT 76
Matt 13:47-50 (included because of Matt   Great net
  13:34-35, 53) // cf. GT 8
Matt 13:52 (included because of Matt 13:34-35,   Householder
  53)
Matt 22:1-10 (cf. Luke 14:15-24) // cf. GT 64   Marriage feast
Matt 22:11-14 (included because of Matt 22:1)   Lack of wedding gar-
                                                       ment
Matt 25:14-30 (Luke 19:11-27—included as a   Talents
  separate parable)

Luke 4:23   Physician, heal your-
                                                       self

Luke 6:39 // Matt 15:14 // cf. GT 34   Blind leading blind
Luke 12:16-21 // cf. GT 63   Rich fool
Luke 12:35 38 (cf. Matt 25:1-13) (included   Watchful servants
  because of Luke 12:41)
Luke 12:39 // Matt 24:43-44 (included because   Thief breaking in
  of Luke 12:41) // cf. GT 21, 103
Luke 13:6-9   Barren fig tree
Luke 14:7-11   Places at a feast
Luke 15:3-7 // Matt 18:12-14 // cf. GT 107   Lost sheep
Luke 18:1-8   Unjust judge
Luke 18:9-14   Pharisee and publican
Luke 19:11-27 (cf. Matt 25:14-30   Pounds

The total number of "parables" in the Gospels in which the term
parabolē is explicitly used or which appear in a collection to which this
term is applied is thirty. Certainly, however, we must enlarge this

listing to include such story and example parables as the parables of the good Samaritan, the prodigal son, etc. It would appear, then, that the following stories found in the Gospels are likewise clearly to be included in any list of parables.

Stories That Are Clearly Parables

Mark 13:34-37 (cf. Matt 25:14-30 // Luke 19:11-27)	Watchful doorkeeper
Matt 18:23-35	Unforgiving servant
Matt 20:1-16	The gracious employer/laborers in vineyard
Matt 21:28-31	Two sons
Matt 24:45-51 // Luke 12:42-46	Wise and foolish servants
Matt 25:1-13 (cf. Luke 12:35-38)	Wise and foolish virgins/Ten virgins
Matt 25:31-46[21]	Sheep and goats
Luke 7:41-43	Two debtors
Luke 10:30-35	Good Samaritan
Luke 11:5-8 (9)	Friend at midnight
Luke 13:25-30 (cf. Matt 25:1-13)	The shut door
Luke 14:15-24 (cf. Matt 22:1-10 which is listed separately) // cf. GT 64	Great supper
Luke 15:8-10 (Note Luke 15:3)	Lost coin
Luke 15:11-32	Gracious father/Prodigal son
Luke 16:1-8	Unjust steward
Luke 16:19-31	Six brothers/Rich man and Lazarus
Luke 17:7-10	Servants' duties

If we add the above seventeen parables to the thirty already listed, we then have a total of forty-seven parables up to this point. There are two other extended comparisons (similitudes) that must be included in any list of parables.

Extended Comparisons Introduced by "Like," "As," or "As If"

Matt 7:24-27 // Luke 6:47-49	Wise and foolish builders
Matt 11:16-19 // Luke 7:31-35	Playing children

At this point the total number of parables is forty-nine. To these are added by various scholars a host of different sayings of Jesus. Rather than making a specific judgment on each of the following passages, we shall simply list them as *possible* examples of parables.

Possible *Parables*

Mark 2:17 // Matt 9:12 // Luke 5:31	Doctor and sick
Mark 2:19-20 // Matt 9:15 // Luke 5:34-35 // cf. GT 104	Wedding guests and fasting
Mark 2:22 // Matt 9:17 // Luke 5:37-38 // cf. GT 47	New wine and old wineskins
Mark 3:27 // Matt 12:29 // Luke 11:21-22 // cf. GT 35	Strong man
Mark 7:27 // Matt 15:26	Children's bread
Mark 9:50 (cf. with Matt 5:13 // Luke 14:34-35)	Tasteless salt
Matt 5:13 // Luke 14:34-35 (cf. with Mark 9:50)	Salt of the earth
Matt 5:14 // cf. GT 32	City on a hill
Matt 5:15 // Luke 11:33 // cf. GT 33	Light under a bushel
Matt 5:25-26 // Luke 12:58-59	Reconciliation with accuser
Matt 6:22-23 // Luke 11:34-36	The sound eye
Matt 6:24 // Luke 16:13 // cf. GT 47	Two masters
Matt 7:3-5 // Luke 6:41-42 // cf. GT 26	Log and speck
Matt 7:6 // cf. GT 93	Pearls before swine
Matt 7:9-11 // Luke 11:11-13	Asking son
Matt 7:16-20 // Luke 6:43-44 // cf. GT 45	Tree and its fruit
Matt 9:37-38 // Luke 10:2 // cf. GT 73	Great harvest
Matt 12:11 // Luke 14:5	Animal in pit
Matt 12:43-45 // Luke 11:24-26	Return of evil spirit
Matt 15:13	Tree not planted by father
Matt 16:2-3 // Luke 12:54-56	Weather signs
Matt 17:25-26	Tribute for earthly kings
Matt 23:25-26 // Luke 11:39-41 // cf. GT 89	Cleansing outside of cup
Matt 24:28 // Luke 17:37	Eagles and body

Luke 14:28-30	Counting cost—tower
Luke 14:31-32	Counting cost—war

It is apparent from the above that it is extremely difficult to determine exactly how many parables we possess in our Gospels. What is clear is that we possess approximately fifty sayings or stories which by any biblical understanding of the term must be called "parables." To these can be added a host of similes and metaphors which might also be included under this designation. What is most evident from this large number found in our Gospels is that Jesus loved to teach using this figure of speech. Why, however, did Jesus choose to teach in parables? It is to this question that we must now turn.

CHAPTER 2

WHY THE PARABLES?

WHY DID JESUS TEACH in parables? At first glance the answer would appear to be self-evident. Parables are earthly stories that illustrate heavenly truths. After all, what better illustration is there of what it means to love one's neighbor than the parable of the good Samaritan? And is there any better illustration of God's gracious and forgiving love than the parable of the prodigal son? Furthermore, the very fact that we have called certain of Jesus' parables "example parables"[1] reveals that some of the parables at least are used to illustrate certain truths. The powerful illustrative nature of Jesus' parables is such that even secular society uses them as illustrations. Yet this view encounters several difficulties not the least of which is the fact that, even for the disciples, the parables were not always self-evident since Jesus frequently had to explain them (MARK 4:13, 34; 7:17). It appears, therefore, that while parables at times reveal and illustrate, they are not always self-evident but at times may even conceal.

THE PARABLE AS A MEANS OF CONCEALING

A most important passage in the Gospels for understanding why Jesus taught in parables is MARK 4:10-12, for here we find an explanation of Jesus' purpose in using this means of proclaiming his message.

> And when he was alone, those who were about him with the twelve asked him concerning the parables. And he said to them, "To you has been given the secret of the kingdom of God, but for those outside everything is in parables; so that they may indeed see but not perceive, and may indeed hear but not understand; lest they should turn again, and be forgiven." (MARK 4:10-12)

The difficulty that these verses raise is obvious, for they appear to say that, rather than seeking to illustrate, the purpose of the parables is to conceal, and the reason for this is more difficult still. The parables are meant to conceal the truth from "those outside" in order to prevent them from understanding and as a result repenting and being forgiven! Many scholars have maintained that such an explanation of why Jesus taught in parables is intolerable and absurd.[2] Furthermore, does not common sense suggest that Jesus, like any teacher or preacher, did not teach to confuse or conceal but to enlighten and reveal? As a result, numerous attempts have been made to explain these verses in ways that would alleviate some of the difficulties.

One such attempt is found in the RSV, where we find the words "so that" in v. 12. In so translating the text, the RSV has implied that not understanding is a *result* of Jesus' teaching in parables rather than the *purpose* or intent of his teaching in this way. The term translated "so that" (*hina*) can be used to describe result ("so that") or purpose ("in order that") as required by the context, and arguments can be made for translating the *hina* in our text as "so that."[3] The basic question is whether the context here requires that the term be translated as implying purpose or result. At first glance the quotation of Isa 6:9-10 in our passage seems to favor the view that *hina* implies purpose here, for the command given to Isaiah reads as follows:

> Go, and say to this people:
> "Hear and hear, but do not understand;
> see and see, but do not perceive."
> Make the heart of this people fat,
> and their ears heavy,
> and shut their eyes;
> lest they see with their eyes,
> and hear with their ears,
> and understand with their hearts,
> and turn and be healed. (Isa 6:9-10)

Yet two things must be observed in regard to the use of this passage in MARK 4:12. First of all, it should be observed that if Jesus (or Mark) had wanted to emphasize the "purpose" nature of the command in Isa 6:9-10, he omitted the single most important part of the command: "Make the heart of this people fat, and their ears heavy, and shut their eyes. . . . " The omission of this part of the quote from Isaiah weakens the "purpose" nature of the Isaiah quotation in MARK 4:12. Secondly, it should be noted that whereas Isa 6:9-10 in its own context does lend itself best to an interpretation which understands that the purpose of Isaiah's preaching was to prevent understanding and repentance,[4] the common interpretation of this passage in Jesus' day saw it as a promise rather than a threat. Nevertheless it must be admitted that the normal way of translating *hina* is as introducing a purpose or final clause ("in order that") rather than as introducing a result or consecutive one ("so that"). The "lest" found in the latter part of MARK 4:12 suggests furthermore that this is probably the way it should be translated here, for "lest" goes better with an "in order that" than with a "so that."

The term "lest," or *mēpote*, found in v. 12 has also been interpreted in several ways. It has been suggested that rather than translating it as "lest" and implying that Jesus taught in parables to prevent his hearers from turning and being forgiven, we should translate the term as "unless" or "if perhaps." Support for this view comes from the fact that the Markan form of the Isa 6:9-10 quotation differs from both the Masoretic and Septuagintal texts and follows rather the form of the text found in the Targums.[5] The Targums, however, translated the *mēpote* of Isa 6:10/MARK 4:12 not as "in order that not," i.e., "lest," but rather as "lest perhaps" or "unless." Rabbinical exegesis therefore took the conclusion of Isa 6:10 as a promise that God would forgive Israel if she repented.[6] If we interpret the *mēpote* in this way, then Jesus' teaching in parables can be interpreted as resulting ("so that") in a lack of understanding which continues "unless" (or "if perhaps," it is hoped) his hearers turn and are forgiven. Certainly this latter interpretation is more attractive, and in Luke 3:15, John 7:26, and 2 Tim 2:25 we have clear examples of *mēpote* meaning "if perhaps." It must be acknowledged, however, that this is not the usual way of translating *mēpote*, and associated with such terms as *hina* ("in order that") and *humin dedotai* ("to you it has been given") in the context of MARK 4:10-12, it raises doubts as to the validity of interpreting the *mēpote* in our passage this way.

Another attempt that has been made to explain these verses is to claim that Mark (or someone before Mark) mistranslated the Aramaic term used by Jesus (*de*) and instead of translating it as "who" (*hoi*), translated it as "in order that" (*hina*).[7] According to this explanation, Jesus originally said something like: "To you has been given the secret of the kingdom of God, but for those outside *who* see but do not perceive and hear but do not understand, everything appears as *mashalim* (riddles or parables)." This explanation, however, has a serious weakness, for it seeks essentially to "save" Jesus by sacrificing Mark! According to this explanation, the problem of these verses lies with Mark (or the pre-Markan tradition), who supposedly mistranslated Jesus' words. One cannot help reflecting on some of the consequences of such an approach, however, before one accepts too readily this particular explanation of the problem. To seek for a canon (what Jesus supposedly said) within a canon (what Mark has actually recorded) has serious consequences. At times it is extremely helpful to be able to arrive at the actual words, or *ipsissima verba*, of Jesus and compare them to the Gospel accounts, for in so doing we have both the words of Jesus and the inspired commentary of those words by the Evangelists. In this instance, however, the words of the Evangelists are rejected as an incorrect interpretation of what we have determined beforehand Jesus could or could not have said. For many, this is not an extremely attractive alternative!

An even clearer attempt to "save" Jesus at the expense of Mark is the denial of the authenticity of MARK 4:10-12.[8] Frequently this passage is seen as a Markan creation that seeks to tie Jesus' teaching in parables with the Evangelist's own theory of the messianic secret and of the divine rejection of Israel.[9] There are, however, a number of reasons for maintaining the authenticity of MARK 4:10-12. Two stylistic features that argue for a Palestinian origin of these verses are the antithetical parallelism in v. 11 and the threefold use of the divine passive ("has been given," "everything is," and "be forgiven"). Most important, however, is the fact that MARK 4:10-12 differs both from the Masoretic and Septuagintal text forms and agrees with the form found in the Targums. This argues strongly in favor of a Palestinian-Aramaic environment for the point of its origin.[10] In the light of the above there is no textual reason for assuming that MARK 4:10-12 is a Markan creation. On the contrary, there is good reason to assume that these verses ultimately go back to Jesus himself.

Still another explanation that has been suggested is that Jesus did in fact speak these words and that the correct translation is "in order that," but it is suggested that in the mind of Jesus, and in the Semitic mind in general, there was little difference between purpose and result in the case of divine decisions.[11] It is suggested that in the Western-oriented world, we usually think from cause to effect. Because of this Greek way of thinking, we then interpret this passage as follows: Since God *purposed* that Jesus' listeners would not repent and be forgiven, Jesus taught in parables and the following *result* was that they did not understand, repent, and receive forgiveness. In contrast it is suggested that the Eastern or Semitic world thought from effect to cause. Thus, this way of thinking would interpret the passage in the following way: Since Jesus' teaching in parables *resulted* in his listeners not understanding and repenting, this must ultimately be due to the *purpose* and plan of God.[12] Because of this latter way of thinking, Jesus could therefore say that he taught in parables "in order that they might indeed see but not perceive, hear but not understand, etc.," even though in his own mind he would have thought primarily from the effect (result) to cause (purpose) rather than from the cause (purpose) to effect (result), i.e., since his listeners did not repent, this must ultimately lie in the divine purpose. This explanation is provocative and does remind us of the constant danger of reading our own way of reasoning and thinking, which is primarily Greek-oriented, into a Semitic culture, but it does not entirely explain away the difficulties of these verses, for such expressions as "to you has been given," "those outside," and "lest" reveal that the lack of understanding-repentance-forgiveness of those outside seems in some way to be intended by God.[13]

The last way of interpreting our passage which we shall mention is to translate the *hina* of MARK 4:12 as an abbreviation for *hina plerōthē* or "in order that it might be fulfilled."[14] We find a good example of this in Matt 18:16, where the quotation of Deut 19:15 is preceded by *hina*, and in Mark 14:49 we find the expression "let the scriptures be fulfilled" in which we find *hina* associated with the verb *plerōthōsin*. If we interpret our passage in this manner, we would then have the following:

> To you has been given the secret of the kingdom of God, but for those outside everything is in parables in order that [what the Scriptures have said may thus be fulfilled and] they may indeed see but not perceive, and may indeed hear but not understand, unless they should turn [in faith to God] and [then they will] be forgiven. (MARK 4:11-12)

Understood in this way, v. 12 is not so much a description of the divine purpose of why Jesus taught in parables as a commentary on the contemporary situation in Jesus' ministry. This interpretation, which is most attractive, is unfortunately also not without its difficulties, for nowhere else in Mark does *hina* by itself introduce an Old Testament quotation.[15] This way of interpreting the *hina* also requires that we interpret the "lest" of v. 12 in the light of the Palestinian Targum's interpretation of Isa 6:9-10 rather than in the light of the Masoretic and Septuagintal text forms, and the legitimacy of this is not certain.

As one can see from the discussion above, numerous "solutions" have been suggested for solving the difficulties found in MARK

4:10-12. As it stands in the Greek text, the meaning of these verses seems fairly clear.[16] The problem does not lie so much in the area of grammar, syntax, and vocabulary as in the area of theology and in Jesus' use of the parables elsewhere. If one accepts a strongly Calvinistic-predestinarian interpretation of v. 12, this does not solve all the problems either, for it is evident that Jesus intentionally used certain parables to teach/reach "those outside" (cf. Luke 15:1-2 and the subsequent parables). It is furthermore evident that at times "those outside" understood the parables of Jesus (cf. MARK 12:12). We have also pointed out that if Jesus (or Mark) really sought to use Isa 6:9-10 as a basis for a strong predestinarian argument, he omitted precisely that part of the Old Testament quotation which would have supported this view, i.e., v. 10, "Make the heart of this people fat, and their ears heavy, and shut their eyes. . . . "

A possible option to this view is the suggestion of J. Arthur Baird that "those outside" are not excluded from understanding all the parables of Jesus but just the parables that deal with the kingdom.[17] Baird points out that approximately two thirds of the parables are explained by Jesus and that few are explained to "those outside." Furthermore, and most importantly, none of the parables explained to those outside deal with the kingdom of God! Baird's thesis has not received the attention that it deserves, for it does appear that Jesus did not explain the kingdom parables to those outside.[18] Yet this thesis also has its weaknesses. For one, what "mystery" do the parables contain which Jesus has not publicly proclaimed in other ways? Is it the fact that the kingdom of God has already come? But one need only note LUKE 11:20; 16:16; Luke 17:20-21; MARK 1:15; etc., to see that elsewhere he has already revealed this to the crowds. The first problem with this thesis is that the parables do not contain anything in them that Jesus had not already shared publicly with "those outside." Secondly, MARK 4:10-12 speaks of "all things" (*ta panta*) being taught in parables to those outside "so that they may indeed see but not perceive. . . . " Verse 11 does not limit the ignorance of those outside to only the secret of the kingdom of God.

If, on the other hand, we accept the more unusual interpretations of *hina* and *mēpote*, we also have several problems. For one, we must realize that the probability of these meaning "so that" or "in order that what the Scriptures say may be fulfilled" and "unless" is considerably less than the probability of either one being interpreted this way.[19] Secondly, it cannot be denied that the parables are not always self-evident illustrations but frequently possess a riddle-like quality, and according to MARK 4:10-12, Jesus intended this. What these verses say about the concealing nature of the parables is also borne out frequently in the life of Jesus. In a number of instances we read that even his disciples did not understand his parables, so that "when he had entered the house, and left the people, his disciples asked him about the parable" (MARK 7:17). Even for the disciples, to whom the secret of the kingdom of God was given, the parables were not always self-evident illustrations. It should also be pointed out in this regard that the most famous Old Testament parable also required an explanation, for it was not until Nathan explained to David, "You are the man" that David understood the meaning of the parable (2 Sam 12:7). It would appear then that Jesus did, at least at times, use the parables for purposes of concealing as well as revealing.[20]

Why Jesus Taught in Parables

Why then did Jesus teach in parables? One reason, according to MARK 4:10-12, was to conceal his teachings from those outside. From even a superficial reading of the Gospels, it is evident that Jesus needed at times to do this. Time and time again Jesus found in his audience those who were hostile toward him. The Sadducees saw in him a threat to their sacerdotal system. His attitudes toward their doctrine (MARK 12:18-27) and above all to the abuse of their role in administering the Temple of God (MARK 11:15-19; cf. 14:58) were a direct threat to their civil and religious authority (MARK 11:27-33; cf. John 11:47-50). Many of the Pharisees likewise saw in Jesus a threat to their own self-righteousness (Luke 18:9-14) and their religious leadership, for Jesus' attack on their hypocrisy (Matt 23:13-36) and the oral traditions (MARK 7:1-13), which they had appended to the law, was bound to bring him into direct conflict with them on numerous issues. Pilate also would have been most suspicious of anyone attracting such large and devoted crowds. This was especially true when Jesus' preaching involved such an easily misunderstood topic as the coming of the kingdom of God. Pilate would have had to ascertain how such a kingdom related to the kingdom of Rome! Furthermore, if in some way the title "Christ" or "Messiah" was being attributed to or discussed with regard to Jesus, this also would have been of great concern to Rome, for the common conception which this title raised was that of a political-military figure who would lead Israel victoriously in battle against her enemies, i.e., Rome.[21]

There was much, therefore, in the message of Jesus that was capable of being misunderstood. By his use of parables Jesus made it more difficult for those who sought to find fault with him and accuse him of sedition. After all, to speak of the kingdom of God as being like a grain of mustard seed (MARK 4:30-32) or like leaven (MATT 13:33) seemed politically quite harmless. By his use of parables Jesus made it difficult for his opponents to bring meaningful charges and accusations against him (cf. MARK 14:55-59). Frequently they would have been confused by the riddle-like quality of the parables. The parables therefore concealed his message to those outside, but privately, after they were explained by Jesus to his followers, they became revealers of his message.

Yet we must be honest and admit that MARK 4:10-12 says more than this. The passage seems to say that Jesus withheld his message from those outside not only in order that they would fail to understand but in order that they would be unable to repent and be forgiven. It must be admitted that this is a most difficult concept. Yet it is obvious that the parables are at times far from self-evident illustrations. We have already pointed out that even the disciples did not always understand them, even though the secret of the kingdom of God was revealed to them. This is evident from the parable of the soils (MARK 4:13; cf. also 7:14-18; Matt 13:36). It will be clear from Chapter 4 that the history of the Christian church also witnesses to the "concealed" nature of the parables, because for centuries their real meanings have been lost through a lack of understanding of the situation of Jesus and through the allegorical method of interpretation.

There are, moreover, other sayings of Jesus which maintain that the message of Jesus was intentionally concealed from certain people.

> At that time Jesus declared, "I thank thee, Father, Lord of heaven and earth, that thou hast hidden these things from the wise and understanding and revealed them to babes; yea, Father, for such was thy gracious will. All things have been delivered to me by my Father; and no one knows the Son except the Father, and no one knows the Father except the Son and any one to whom the Son chooses to reveal him." (MATT 11:25-27)

Here as in MARK 4:10-12 we encounter a similar teaching that understanding and faith are a divine gift, and Paul in Rom 11:25-32 explains the unbelief of his people in part at least as due to a divine hardening by God, so that as a result the message of salvation might be extended to the Gentiles. It may be unwarranted to see Rom 11:25-32 as a commentary of MARK 4:10-12,[22] but in its present form MARK 4:10-12 seems to say that one of the reasons Jesus taught in parables was to conceal his message from "those outside."

Another reason why Jesus taught in parables appears to conflict with the first, for a second reason was to reveal and illustrate his message to both his followers and "those outside." The parables are frequently most effective illustrations of Jesus' message. For the original lawyer as well as for every reader since, the parable of the good Samaritan illustrates in an unforgettable way what it means to be a loving neighbor, and if one sought an example to illustrate the gracious love of God for sinners, where could one find a better one than the parable of the prodigal son? The parables of Jesus were/are excellent illustrations of his message and this was/is especially true for those to whom the secret of the kingdom of God has been given, but at times even those "outside" did not and could not miss the point Jesus was seeking to illustrate in the parable.

> And they tried to arrest him, but feared the multitude, for they perceived that he had told the parable against them; so they left him and went away. (MARK 12:12)

A third and final reason why Jesus taught in parables that we shall mention was to disarm his listeners. At times Jesus sought to penetrate the hostility and hardness of heart of his listeners by means of a parable. The famous parable of Nathan in 2 Sam 12:1-4 is a perfect Old Testament example of this. How was Nathan to bring to David's attention the fact of his sin and God's anger over it? If he sought to confront David directly with his adultery, David might have hardened his heart and as a result placed a barrier between himself and the Word of the Lord. Therefore, Nathan shrewdly used a parable and David became so involved with the parable that he was horrified over the injustice and evil that had been done. Then when David's heart was open and he was disarmed of any defense mechanisms, Nathan gave the interpretation of the parable. Now the Word of the Lord, unhindered by the armor of a hard heart, pierced the soul of David and he was convicted of his sin. The parable worked, and David repented. We find a similar use of a parable by Jesus in Luke 7:36-50. Here, in order to pierce through Simon's hardness of heart and prejudice, Jesus spoke in a parable and sought to reach Simon. Jesus even involved Simon in the parable and in so doing, it is hoped, made him ask himself, "Is my lack of great love due to a lack of real forgiveness?" Other examples of this use of parables are found in Luke 15, where Jesus, by the trilogy of parables, seeks to explain the protest of Luke 15:1-2.[23]

CHAPTER 3

WHENCE THE PARABLES?

IN OUR INVESTIGATION of the origin of the parables, we shall arrange our discussion under three headings. The first involves the geographical locale out of which the parables arose; the second deals with the question of the authenticity of the parables; and the third concerns the nature of the material found in the parables.

THE GEOGRAPHICAL LOCALE OF THE PARABLES

It is evident as one investigates the parables that they bear a distinctly Palestinian, and at times even Galilean, flavor.[1] As one reads the parables, it is also apparent that they arose in a rural environment, and if one investigates the parables more carefully it becomes clear that this rural environment must be Palestine and at times the region of Galilee.

The parable of the sower and the seed (MARK 4:2-20) is a good example of this. The parable presents a number of questions to the reader, not the least of which is how the sower of the parable can be so wasteful. How can any farmer sow his seed indiscriminately on paths, in weeds, on rocks, and on good soil? Such wastefulness is sheer foolishness! Clearly, by modern standards, Jesus chose a most inept farmer for his example. Yet upon closer examination, the difficulty we encounter in the practice of the farmer arises primarily out of our ignorance of Palestinian farming practices, for in Palestine the sowing of the seed preceded the plowing. We find examples of this practice in the Pseudepigrapha[2] as well as in the Talmud, for in the latter it is expressly stated that in Palestine the farmer sows first and then plows and the following order is given: sowing, plowing, reaping.[3] The passage also gives the distinct impression that this was not the usual order in other areas. The sower of Jesus' parable was simply doing what any farmer would do in Palestine. The path made by various people walking across the field would be plowed shortly; the weeds would soon be plowed under; and the fact is that in Palestine it is not always easy to tell where the ground is rocky, for there is usually a thin layer of soil covering the underlying limestone. The parable of the sower and the soils therefore clearly betrays the practice of farming in Palestine.

Another example of the Palestinian, and to be more precise the Galilean, flavor of some of the parables is the parable of the evil tenants (MARK 12:1-11). The parable has been criticized at times for being unrealistic, for why would the tenants of the vineyard ever think that by killing the son they would possess the vineyard? It has been pointed out, however, that in the unique context of Galilee, where absentee landlords were not uncommon and where there was much agrarian and revolutionary unrest, the parable makes good sense.[4] Since the owner lived elsewhere (cf. MARK 12:1, he departed), such treatment of the servants by the tenants was conceivable, and the arrival of the son might have been construed as indicating that he was now the new heir upon the death of his father and that he had now come to renew the lease. His death might leave the vineyard ownerless and thus the land might become theirs, for "possession is nine tenths of the law," and who would have any better opportunity to possess ownerless land than the tenants who were presently residing on the property?[5] At the very least such a death might provide a respite from the payment of rent! The parable therefore reflects well the social environment of Galilee in Jesus' day where the dispossessed tenant farmers were in a constant state of agitation toward their foreign absentee landlords on whose estates they served. It is not surprising, therefore, to learn that Galilee was a hotbed of revolution and discontent and that the founder of the Zealot sect, according to Josephus,[6] was Judas the Galilean!

Other parables also betray a Palestinian locale. Certainly the presence of such terms as "priest," "Levite," and "Samaritan," as well as the scene (the road between Jerusalem and Jericho), indicates that the parable of the good Samaritan (Luke 10:30-35) would have arisen in Palestine. The reference to the Pharisee, the publican, and the Temple (Luke 18:9-14) also indicates that this parable must have arisen in Palestine. The parable of the great net (Matt 13:47-50), while capable of being understood in an environment apart from the sea, is far more likely to have been uttered in a fishing environment, and the distinction between good and bad fish can best be understood in a Jewish situation in which certain fish were good or clean and bad or unclean.[7] What more likely place can one imagine for telling such a parable than the region around the Sea of Galilee? Two other parables that can best be understood in a Palestinian context are the parables of the laborers in the vineyard (Matt 20:1-16) and the wise and foolish virgins (Matt 25:1-13). In the former we should note that the work is performed by hired servants. Outside of Palestine farm work was usually performed by slaves, whereas in Palestine the work was still performed by hired laborers. Furthermore, payment of wages at the end of the day was customary in Palestine, based on Lev 19:13 and Deut 24:14-15.[8] With regard to the latter parable, the lamplight procession of the bridegroom and bride from the house of the bride to the house of the bridegroom's parents fits well the information we have concerning Jewish weddings during this period.[9] Only a radical skepticism would therefore deny that the most natural point of origin for the parables is to be found in the teaching ministry of Jesus in Palestine and, at times even more specifically, in Galilee.

THE AUTHENTICITY OF THE PARABLES

From the above it is evident that the parables found in our Gospels arose in a Jewish environment located in Palestine. To be more explicit, we can say that some of the parables had their place of origin in Galilee. Yet it might be argued that the parables could have arisen in the Palestinian/Galilean church after the death and resurrection of Jesus and then read back upon his lips. Few New Testament scholars today would hold such a radical view, however, for there are two additional arguments that further support the authenticity of the New Testament parables.

One argument is the fact that the parables meet the "criterion of dissimilarity" or "distinctiveness." The criterion of dissimilarity maintains that if a teaching (or in this case both the teaching and the form of the teaching) attributed to Jesus in our Gospels could not have derived either from the Judaism of Jesus' day or from the early church, it must be authentic, i.e., it must stem from Jesus himself. This tool, used widely in recent life and teachings of Jesus research, has certain weaknesses, but it is nevertheless helpful in establishing a minimum of authentic material that scholars are willing to accept as authentic.[10] The parables in our Gospels meet this criterion nicely in that we find no parables anywhere else in the New Testament or in the earliest writings of the church fathers, so that it is difficult to think that the parables were created by the early church and then read back upon the lips of Jesus.[11] We furthermore find nothing like these parables in the intertestamental literature of Judaism.[12] As a result, it is clear that the gospel parables must stem from Jesus himself.

The second argument in favor of the authenticity of the parables is the fact that both their content and language agree with that found in other sayings of Jesus which scholars agree were uttered by Jesus. There is a consensus among New Testament scholars today that such themes as the kingdom of God, the Fatherhood of God, the offer of the kingdom of God to publicans and sinners, the call for radical decision, the emphasis on the attitude of the heart rather than merely external appearance, were an integral part of the proclamation of Jesus, and these are the very themes that appear constantly in the parables of Jesus.[13]

While it is true that many scholars believe that the gospel parables have experienced various modifications and interpretations by the early church and the Evangelists, because of the above there is almost universal agreement that in the parables we stand on the firm foundation of Jesus' own teachings.[14]

The Nature of the Material in the Parables

In reading the parables, one becomes impressed with their down-to-earth, real-life character. No doubt we must see in them various experiences and observations of Jesus as a child, youth, and young man in Nazareth. The different results that a farmer had in his sowing of the seed reminded him later of his own experience in "sowing the word" (MARK 4:2-20). The smallness of the mustard seed in contrast to its final growth as a large shrub impressed him. Later on he could not help comparing this with the small beginning of his mission. Yes, the kingdom of God was like a mustard seed. How small was its beginning. How insignificant in the eyes of Rome and the world. Yet when God brought about its consummation, how great it would be (MARK 4:30-32). It has even been suggested by some that the parable of the lost coin (Luke 15:8-10) may have arisen from an experience in Jesus' own home when his mother lost a coin! The beauty of the lily (MATT 6:28-30), the foolishness of the man who built his home carelessly on a poor foundation (MATT 7:24-27), perhaps a recent experience in which a man purchased a field in which he found a treasure (Matt 13:44), etc., were firmly etched in his mind and later became the metaphors in which he would clothe his message. No doubt the common pool of wisdom sayings and *mashalim* that circulated in Palestine in the first century served as sources upon which he could draw as well.

While it is evident that the materials for Jesus' parables came out of the real world of the historical Jesus, this does not necessarily mean that they are all realistic in the sense of being true to life. The story is told of a pastor in a large city who counseled a modern-day prodigal to return home to his father, for if he did, his father would surely forgive him and "kill the fatted calf" (Luke 15:23). The young man did as the pastor counseled and some time later the pastor saw him again and in his excitement asked the young man how things went. "Did he kill the fatted calf?" he asked. To this the young man replied, "No, but he just about killed the prodigal son!" Not all fathers are like the father of Jesus' parable. All too often finding such a father who reflects the divine love and forgiveness is a rare and unique experience. Generous owners such as we find in the parable of the laborers in the vineyard (Matt 20:1-16) are also few and far between, and not all priests, Levites, or Samaritans were like the ones portrayed in the parable of the good Samaritan!

When we say, therefore, that the parables arose out of normal life situations, this does not mean that the parables simply portray normal, everyday behavior. On the contrary, at times Jesus' parables caught their listeners by surprise because the behavior they expected stood in sharp contrast with the behavior portrayed in the parables. A good example of this can be found in the parable of the dishonest steward (Luke 16:1-8). This parable was understandable to its hearers because it was cast in the real-world imagery of its audience (rich man, stewards, accounts, debtors, etc.). The commendation of the dishonest steward by the rich man, however, was clearly not normal, everyday behavior and no doubt caught the hearers by surprise. We also find hyperbolic exaggeration at times in Jesus' use of numbers. In the parable of the unforgiving servant Jesus speaks of one servant being forgiven ten thousand talents (Matt 18:24). When we realize that the entire yearly tribute of Galilee and Peraea in 4 B.C. was only two hundred talents[15] and that the entire annual income of Herod the Great was only nine hundred talents,[16] we can see how exaggerated the sum Jesus used really is. And it must likewise be admitted that it would be quite unusual for all ten maidens to be asleep when the bridegroom finally came (Matt 25:5).

To claim that Jesus' parables are drawn from real life does not therefore mean that they do not at times portray unusual features. What is meant by the real-life nature of Jesus' parables is that unlike fables, they do not envision an unreal world where trees talk, people fly like birds, animals write books, etc. The parables of Jesus use everyday scenes and experiences, and although at times they exhibit unusual features, they are understandable in the light of everyday experiences. As a result, although it is highly unusual that all the invited guests in the parable of the great supper would make excuses for not coming to the banquet (LUKE 14:18), the scene itself is an understandable real-life situation.

In concluding this chapter we must allude briefly to the artistic character and genius of the parables. Jesus was a master storyteller. The appeal of Jesus' parables for over nineteen centuries is due not only to their authoritative revelation of the character and will of God but also in part to their artistic quality. We shall refer at times to this quality in later chapters, but a few examples must be pointed out here. Jesus had the ability to create vivid portraits and scenes. How does one describe the plight of a young man who, having squandered his fortune, now finds himself destitute and starving? Jesus describes this young Jewish man as being in a far country, having "joined" himself to a Gentile, feeding the forbidden pigs for a job, and wishing that he could fill his stomach by sharing the "table" of the pigs he fed, etc. The description is most vivid and memorable! And the portrayal of the prodigal's father running, embracing, kissing his lost son, ignoring his son's words of repentance, and ordering that he be clothed with the best robe, sandals, and a ring surely creates an unforgettable portrait of the great love of God. Jesus also knew how to heighten the suspense and tension in telling a parable. It is not simply coincidence that those who worked all day are paid last in the parable of the gracious employer. It is also not merely coincidental that the characters portrayed in the parable of the good Samaritan are a priest, a Levite, and a Samaritan. As we study the parables, it becomes increasingly clear how brilliantly Jesus used the parables as effective tools for conveying his message.

CHAPTER 4

HOW THE PARABLES
WERE INTERPRETED

IT HAS BEEN SAID often that the ignorance of history dooms one to repeat its mistakes, for a knowledge of the past reveals to us the mistakes that we should avoid in the future as well as the successes that we should emulate. In seeking to understand how to interpret the parables of Jesus, we can learn a great deal from the ways in which the parables have been interpreted throughout church history. Our discussion of *how* to interpret the parables will be divided into two chapters. The first will deal with parabolic interpretation from the earliest church fathers until the modern period (A.D. 1888). Here we shall look at the ruling method of interpreting that dominated the Christian church—the allegorical method. In the next chapter we shall look at the insights that have been gained into how to interpret the parables since the appearance of Adolf Jülicher's great work, *Die Gleichnisreden Jesu*, in 1888.

The Period of the Early Church Fathers (to A.D. 540)

During this period of the early church the allegorical method of interpreting the parables came to dominate the scene. No doubt the early church fathers were greatly influenced in this by the fact that for centuries it was popular to allegorize the heroes of Homer and their actions in order to satisfy the scruples of the morally sensitive. Allegory was the means by which the actions of these ancient heroes, whose morality and standards were no longer acceptable, could be adapted and still be useful to later generations. This method was later used by the Jewish scholar Philo as a means of demonstrating that the teachings of the Old Testament were in perfect harmony with the teachings of

Greek philosophy which he had accepted. The early church, therefore, had a ready-made tool which it could use for similar purposes, and it is not surprising, therefore, to observe that the early church fathers who came out of a Greek milieu proceeded to apply this method to the interpretation of the Scriptures. Various Old Testament passages that appeared to be unacceptable to them were simply allegorized, so that a "deeper," more acceptable meaning could be found that was "Christian." It need only be mentioned that this is still done at times today. Many Christians, for example, throughout the history of the church (this holds also for Judaism) have found the literal meaning of the Song of Songs as either unacceptable or at least inadequate. As a result, the "true" or "deeper" meaning was seen as an allegory of the love of Christ for the church (or of Yahweh for Israel)! Furthermore, the fact that certain parables are given an allegorical interpretation in the Gospels themselves (cf. MARK 4:3-9 with 4:13-20; Matt 13:24-29 with 13:36-43) no doubt gave the impression to many that all the parables were to be treated in this manner.[1]

In the light of the above, it is not surprising that the allegorical method was used quite extensively by the early church in the interpretation of the parables of Jesus. One of the earliest examples of the use of allegory is found in the writings of Marcion (d. 160). According to Marcion, the good Samaritan (Luke 10:30-35) was actually Jesus, who appeared for the first time in history between Jerusalem and Jericho as the good Samaritan.[2] It is not important for us to know exactly why or how Marcion came to such an allegorical interpretation, but such an interpretation did fit well with his docetic teachings because it permitted him to deny the incarnation and true humanity of Jesus. What is important to note is that the earliest known reference to the parable of the good Samaritan treated the parable allegorically as teaching a Christological doctrine rather than literally as teaching an ethical attitude!

In the writings of Irenaeus (ca. 130-ca. 200) we possess several examples of the allegorical method of interpretation. In his treatment of the laborers in the vineyard (Matt 20:1-16),[3] he interpreted the first call to work as referring to those whom God called at the beginning of creation. Those who received the second call (third hour) were "after this," i.e., those who lived under the old covenant; those who received the third call (sixth hour) were those present "after the middle of time" or those present during the ministry of Jesus; those receiving the fourth call (ninth hour) were Irenaeus' contemporaries; and those who received the last call (eleventh hour) were those who would be present at the end time. The vineyard, furthermore, was seen as representing righteousness, the householder as representing the Spirit of God, and the denarius as representing the knowledge of the Son of God which is immortality. The parable of the hidden treasure (Matt 13:44) is also treated allegorically, for Irenaeus concluded that the field symbolized the Scriptures and the treasure symbolized Christ.[4] The good Samaritan is treated in a similar manner,[5] for the good Samaritan refers to Christ, who had compassion and bound up the wounds of the man who fell among thieves, and the two denarii represent the "image and inscription of the Father and the Son."

Tertullian (ca.160-ca.220), despite some excellent insights into parabolic interpretation,[6] also interpreted the parables allegorically. This can be seen in his treatment of the parable of the gracious father (Luke 15:11-32). Tertullian interpreted this parable in the following way: the older son represents the Jew who is envious of the divine offer of salvation to the Gentile; the father represents God; the younger son represents the Christian; the inheritance that was squandered represents the wisdom and natural ability to know God which man possesses as his birthright; the citizen in the far country represents the devil; the swine represent the demons; the robe represents the sonship which Adam lost through his transgression; the ring represents Christian baptism; the feast represents the sacrament of the Lord's Supper; and the fatted calf slain for the prodigal represents the Savior present at the Lord's Supper.[7]

A contemporary of Irenaeus and Tertullian was Clement of Alexandria (ca.150-ca.215). Clement follows the Alexandrian herme-neutical tradition and allegorizes the parable of the good Samaritan more fully than anyone previous. Clement gives the following interpretation of the parable:

> Good Samaritan = Neighbor = Christ
> Thieves = Rulers of darkness
> Wounds = Fears, lusts, wraths, pains, de-
> ceits, pleasures
> Wine = Blood of David's vine
> Oil = Compassion of the Father
> Binding [of health = Love, faith, hope[8]
> and of salvation]

Clement's successor as head of the catechetical school in Alexandria was Origen (ca. 184-ca. 254). It is uncertain as to how much Origen may have been influenced by Clement, but the allegorical tendency we found in Clement became a science with Origen. Origen maintained that the Scriptures possessed a threefold sense even as man, according to 1 Thess 5:23, possessed a threefold nature. Even as man, according to Origen's interpretation of this passage, contained a body, soul, and spirit, so also did the Scriptures possess a body or the *literal* sense of the text (which was primarily for those people unable to arrive at the deeper meaning, i.e., the uneducated[9]), a soul or the *moral* (also called the tropological) sense of the text, and a spirit or the *spiritual* sense of the text.[10] Thus, the mustard seed in the parable of the mustard seed (MARK 4:30-32) refers at the same time to an actual mustard seed (the literal sense), to faith (the moral sense), and to the kingdom of God (the spiritual sense). Like Irenaeus, Origen also allegorized the laborers in the vineyard (Matt 20:1-16). For Origen, however, the first call referred to those alive between Creation and Noah, the second call to those alive between Noah and Abraham, the third call as those alive between Abraham and Moses, the fourth call as those between Moses and Joshua, the fifth call as those between Joshua and the time of Christ. The householder was also seen as representing God and the denarius, salvation.

When Origen applied this method of interpretation to the parable of the good Samaritan, he arrived at the following:

```
The man going down = Adam
         to Jericho
Jerusalem from which = Paradise
       he was going
             Jericho = The world
             Robbers = Hostile influences and enemies of man
                       such as the thieves and murderers
                       mentioned in John 10:8
              Wounds = Disobedience or sins
               Priest = Law
               Levite = Prophets
      Good Samaritan = Christ
                Beast = Body of Christ
                  Inn = Church
          Two denarii = Knowledge of the Father and the Son
           Innkeeper = Angels in charge of the church
       Return of the = Second coming of Christ[11]
      Good Samaritan
```

Although Origen's allegorical treatment of Scripture in general met substantial opposition,[12] the allegorical interpretation gained strength.

Other church fathers continued to allegorize the parable of the good Samaritan. Ambrose of Milan (339-390) also saw the good Samaritan as a reference to Christ,[13] but the man's going down from Jerusalem to Jericho was seen as a reference not to the fall of Adam but to the Christian's shrinking back from a martyr's conflict to the pleasures and comforts of this world. As for the robbers, these represented the persecutors of the church. It is with Augustine (354-430), however, that the allegorization of this parable reaches its high point in the early church. According to Augustine, the parable was to be interpreted as follows:

The man going down to Jericho	= Adam
Jerusalem from which he was going	= City of Heavenly Peace
Jericho	= The moon which signifies our mortality (there is a play here on the Hebrew terms for moon and Jericho)
Robbers	= Devil and his angels
Stripping him	= Taking away his immortality
Beating him	= Persuading him to sin
Leaving him half dead	= Due to sin, he was dead spiritually, but half alive, due to his knowledge of God
Priest	= Priesthood of the Old Testament (Law)
Levite	= Ministry of the Old Testament (Prophets)
Good Samaritan	= Christ
Binding of the wounds	= Restraint of sin
Oil	= Comfort of good hope
Wine	= Exhortation to spirited work
Beast	= Body of Christ
Inn	= Church
Two denarii	= Two commandments of love
Innkeeper	= Apostle Paul
Return of the Good Samaritan	= Resurrection of Christ[14]

From the above it is evident that the allegorical method was the dominating way in which the parables of Jesus were interpreted in the early church. This is revealed quite clearly by the vast geographical area in which this method reigned: Irenaeus (Lyons); Tertullian

(Carthage); Clement (Alexandria); Origen (Alexandria, Caesarea); Ambrose (Milan); Augustine (Hippo). There was some protest in the early church against this method of interpretation, especially from the church fathers in Antioch. Men like Isidore of Pelusium (360-435), Basil (ca.329-379), Theodore of Mopsuestia (350?-428), and Chrysostom (349-407) protested against the allegorical method. The latter even said that it was neither wise nor correct "to inquire curiously into all things in parables word by word, but when we have learnt the object for which it was composed, to read this, and not to busy one's self about anything further."[15] At best, however, such protests were simply voices crying in the wilderness, for the allegorical method of interpretation clearly dominated not only the interpretation of the parables but all biblical interpretation as well.

The Middle Ages (540-1500)

Whereas the main emphasis of the early church fathers lay in the area of biblical exegesis, the main concern of the Scholastics during the Middle Ages lay in the area of systematic theology, and it was during this particular period that complex theological systems arose. In general, the Scholastics of this period relied rather heavily upon the exegetical work of the early church fathers. To Origen's threefold sense of Scripture, however, they now added still another which they called the anagogical. As a result, in addition to Origen's *literal, moral,* and *spiritual* (now called simply the allegorical) meanings, there was also the *anagogical* meaning which sought the heavenly or eschatological meaning of the text.[16] A well-known example of this type of interpretation was the fourfold meaning contained in the term "Jerusalem." In the literal sense, Jerusalem was understood to refer to a specific city in Judea; in the moral or tropological sense it referred to the human soul; in the spiritual or allegorical sense it referred to the church; and in the anagogical sense it referred to the heavenly abode of the saints.[17]

In their interpretation of the parable of the good Samaritan, the Scholastics were clearly debtors to the work of the early church fathers. For instance, when we read the Venerable Bede (673-735), it appears that we are once again reading Augustine, for we discover the following:

The man going down = Adam
         to Jericho
Jerusalem from which = City of Heavenly Peace
         he is going

Jericho = Moon which signifies variation and
change
Robbers = Devil and his angels
Stripping him = Stripping Adam of his glorious vestment
of immortality and innocence
Wounds = Sins
Priest = Priesthood of the Old Testament
Levite = Ministry of the Old Testament
Samaritan = Christ
Oil = Repentance
Beast = The flesh in which the Lord came to us,
i.e., the incarnation
Etc.[18]

Along with the Venerable Bede could also be mentioned Theophylactus (1050-1108), Bernard of Clairvaux (1090-1153), Bonaventure
(1217-1274), and many others who continued to interpret this parable
along allegorical and Christological lines.[19]

The last representative of the Middle Ages that we shall mention is
Thomas Aquinas (1226-1274). Aquinas defended the allegorical method
of interpretation and the fourfold meaning of the text in his great work,
Summa Theologica.[20] Aquinas' interpretation of the parable of the good
Samaritan in *Catena Aurea* is an especially valuable source for ascertaining
the prevailing method of theological interpretation of this parable, for his
commentary on the parable is essentially a compendium of scholastic
and earlier allegorical interpretations. Actually, Aquinas did little
original work on the exegesis of this parable. What he primarily does is to
quote with approval the exegetical work of men like Augustine,
Pseudo-Augustine, Cyril, Basil, Chrysostom, Gregory the Great, the
Venerable Bede, Theophylactus, and others. The result is therefore not
unexpected, for his interpretation of such terms as man, Jericho,
Jerusalem, robbers, wounds, priest, Levite, Samaritan, beast, is
essentially Augustinian. At times Aquinas even places side by side
different opinions as to what the allegorical significance of a term may be
without commenting as to which he himself believes to be the correct
one. An example of this is the significance of the terms "wine" and "oil"
in the parable. After quoting Augustine, who interprets them to mean
the "comfort of good hope" and the "exhortation to spirited work"
respectively, he proceeds to quote Gregory the Great, who interprets
them as the "sharpness of constraint" and the "softness of mercy," as
well as Theophylactus, who interprets them as "intercourse with God"
and "intercourse with men."[21]

THE REFORMATION AND POST-REFORMATION PERIOD 1500-1888

The Reformation brought with it new insights on how to interpret the Scriptures. Martin Luther (1483-1546) renounced the medieval conception of the fourfold sense of Scripture and likened the allegorizers of Scripture to "clerical jugglers performing monkey tricks (Affenspiel)."[22] The Scriptures, for Luther, contained basically one meaning, and that meaning was to be found in the literal sense. Other types of interpretation, regardless of how appealing they might be, were simply the work of fools! It is not surprising, therefore, to observe that Luther especially disapproved of the exegetical work of Origen and considered his exegesis as "worth less than dirt."[23] For Luther, the Scriptures were to be interpreted literally, i.e., grammatically, not allegorically. Whereas Luther was sound in regard to theory, his practice unfortunately was not always consistent with his theory in that he tended to allegorize the parables and find everywhere in them examples of the doctrine of justification by faith. A good example of his allegorical interpretation of the parables is his interpretation of the parable of the good Samaritan. On several occasions he refers to this parable and interprets it as follows:

> The man going down = Adam and all mankind
> to Jericho
> Robbers = Devils who robbed and wounded us
> Priest = Fathers (Noah, Abraham) before Moses
> Levite = Priesthood of the Old Testment
> Good Samaritan = Lord Jesus Christ
> Oil/Wine = Whole Gospel from beginning to end
> Oil = Grace
> Wine = Cross Christian called to bear
> Beast = Christ the Lord
> Inn = Christianity in world (church)
> Innkeeper = Preacher of the Word of God[24]

Clearly, the best and most consistent exegete of all the Reformers was John Calvin (1509-1564), whose commentaries contain many lasting insights and still reward their readers. Like Luther, Calvin protested against the allegorical method of interpretation, and he referred to the allegorizing of the early church as "idle fooleries." It is not surprising, therefore, to find in his works the first explicit rejection of the Christological interpretation of the parable of the good Samaritan. In his *A Harmony of the Gospels Matthew, Mark and Luke,* Calvin states:

An allegorical interpretation devised by proponents of free will is
really too futile to deserve an answer. According to them, under
the figure of a wounded man is described the condition of Adam
after the fall. Whence they infer that the power to act well was not
quite extinct, for he is only said to be half-dead. As if Christ would
have intended to speak here about the corruption of human
nature, and discuss whether the wound Satan struck on Adam
was fatal or curable; as if He had not plainly declared, without any
figurative talk, that all are dead unless He quickens them with His
voice (John 5:25). I give as little respect for that other allegory
which has won such regard that nearly everyone comes down in
its favour like an oracle. In this, they make out the Samaritan to be
Christ, because He is our protector: they say that wine mixed with
oil was poured into the wound because Christ heals us with
repentance and the promise of grace. And a third cunning story
has been made up, that Christ does not immediately restore health
but sends us to the Church, that is the inn-keeper, to be cured
gradually. None of these strikes me as plausible: we should have
more reverence for Scripture than to allow ourselves to transfigure
its sense so freely. Anyone may see that these speculations have
been cooked up by meddlers, quite divorced from the mind of
Christ.[25]

In rejecting the allegorical interpretation of this parable, Calvin reveals
not only his great exegetical insight but his courage and integrity as
well, in that during the previous fifteen centuries we know of no one
who explicitly rejected the allegorical/Christological interpretation of
this parable! The chief aim of the parable for Calvin is "to show that
neighbourliness which obliges us to do our duty by each other is not
restricted to friends and relations, but open to the whole human
race."[26] Elsewhere, Calvin shows the same insight with regard to how
the parables should be interpreted. In discussing the parable of the
unjust steward (Luke 16:1-8), he warns against pressing the details for
meaning but seeks a single point and meaning for the parable.[27]

Likewise in his discussion of the parable of the gracious employer
(Matt 20:1-6) Calvin states:

To want to examine the details of this parable precisely would be
empty curiosity. We should look for nothing more than Christ
intended to tell us.[28]

With such insights it is obvious that Calvin's methodology for
interpreting the parables was clearly centuries ahead of his time.

Unfortunately, the successors of Luther and Calvin did not follow their sound hermeneutical principles, and, in the case of Calvin especially, his sound hermeneutical practice,[29] for their insights into the interpretation of the Scriptures were soon forgotten. Melanchthon, for instance, continued to interpret the parable of the good Samaritan in essentially the same manner that Augustine did,[30] so that Jerusalem referred to Paradise, Jericho to the moon, the man to Adam, the robbers to the devil, the Samaritan to Christ, etc.

Even in the nineteenth century the allegorical method of interpretation continued to dominate the interpretation of the parables. Perhaps the single most influential work on the parables published in the nineteenth century in the English-speaking world was Archbishop R. C. Trench's *Notes on the Parables of Our Lord,* which was published in 1841. After a careful exegetical analysis in which he interprets the parable in the context of the time and situation of Jesus and emphasizes the ethical dimension of the parable, Trench seeks to obtain the "deeper" meaning of the parable and allegorizes the parable as follows:

The man going down to Jericho	= Human nature or Adam
Jerusalem from which he was going	= Heavenly city
Jericho	= Profane city, a city under a curse
Robbers	= Devil and his angels
Stripping him	= Stripping him of his original robe of righteousness
Leaving him half dead	= Covered with almost moral strokes, every sinful passion and desire a gash from which the lifeblood of his soul is flowing—yet still maintaining a divine spark which might be fanned into flame
Priest and Levite	= Inability of the Law to save
Good Samaritan	= Christ
Binding of wounds	= Sacraments, which heal the wounds of the soul
Oil	= Christ in the human heart purifying the heart by faith—the anointing of the Holy Spirit
Wine	= Blood of Christ's passion
Placing man on beast and walking alongside	= "Reminds us of him, who, though he was rich, yet for our sakes became poor"

Inn = Church
Two denarii = All gifts and graces, sacraments,
                     powers of healing, of remission of
                     sins
Whatever more you = Reward for righteous service [31]
        spend

It is evident that Trench was far more influenced by Origen and Augustine than by Calvin!

CONCLUSION

From the brief survey of the history of parabolic interpretation just given, it is obvious that the allegorical method of interpretation dominated the way in which the Christian church interpreted the parables. To be sure, there were occasional protests raised against this methodology by the Antiochene School and by Luther and Calvin. The latter especially had a most perceptive grasp of how the parables should be interpreted, but Calvin, Luther, and the Antiochene School did not succeed in overturning the predominant use of allegory in interpreting the parables. Even if the Reformer's protest against the fourfold meaning of Scripture was acknowledged as correct, when it came to the parables the literal meaning was not enough. It was the "deeper" or allegorical meaning of the text which was most desired. It would not be until 1888 that the chain of allegorical interpretation which bound the parables would once and for all be broken.

CHAPTER 5

HOW THE PARABLES
ARE INTERPRETED

WITHIN THE LAST CENTURY several major advances have taken place in the investigation of the parables of Jesus. As a result we can today sense better than ever before what Jesus intended to teach and do through his parables. In this chapter we shall investigate the contributions made to the interpretation of the parables by the following: Adolf Jülicher; C. H. Dodd and Joachim Jeremias; redaction criticism; and some of the more recent authors. We shall seek to formulate certain basic principles which we can use as guides for the interpretation of the parables of Jesus in the next chapters.

ADOLF JÜLICHER

The modern period of parable interpretation began with the publication of Adolf Jülicher's first volume of *Die Gleichnisreden Jesu* in 1888. Up to 1888 the allegorical method reigned supreme in the interpretation of the parables. With the publication of this work the allegorical captivity of the parables ended once and for all. Jülicher demonstrated in an irrefutable way that the parables were not allegories. In contrast to an allegory, which he defined as a series of metaphors in which each metaphor has its own meaning and significance, Jülicher defined a parable as a similitude which has only a single point of comparison *(tertium comparationis)*. Each parable is therefore a single picture which seeks to portray a single object or reality. The details of the picture (parable) as a result do not serve any function in and of themselves but simply provide background or give coloring for the single point or reality which the picture is seeking to portray.

When we apply this understanding to the parable of the good Samaritan, it becomes clear that it is unimportant that the man was going down from Jerusalem to Jericho. He could just as easily have been going up from Jericho to Jerusalem! This would in no way alter the one point of comparison. Likewise, the "two denarii" have no particular significance for the point of the parable. It could just as easily have been three! (One cannot help pausing for a moment to muse over how Origen and some of the early church fathers would have interpreted "three denarii.") As for the wine and the oil, again there is no other level of meaning or reality that these terms seek to convey. They are simply part of the local coloring of the story, for wine served an antiseptic function in washing the wounds and oil would aid in keeping the wounds open and thus allow them to drain. If we interpret this parable as Jülicher suggests, we shall simply seek to ascertain the one basic point of comparison found in the parable rather than to place a great deal of emphasis upon the details. That point involves the behavior of the Samaritan in general, not in any single aspect of that behavior or of the story. We must therefore recognize that the point of the parable lies not in a review of salvation history but rather in the acting neighborly of the good Samaritan.

Jülicher's main contribution to the investigation of the parables was that he pointed out the difference between parables and allegories and in so doing laid to rest once and for all the allegorical method of interpretation that had plagued the church for centuries. It is now clear that parables are not allegories, as Origen, Augustine, and others thought, because a parable is for the most part an extended simile or metaphor and has, therefore, only one *tertium comparationis*, whereas an allegory is a chain or series of metaphors.

Jülicher's work, despite its great contribution to the interpretation of the parables, was not, however, without its own limitations. The first major limitation of Jülicher was that he overreacted against the former emphasis on the allegorical interpretation of the parables and denied the presence of any allegorical element in the parables of Jesus. Whenever such allegorical details or interpretations were present in the Gospels, their authenticity was denied, and they were attributed to the reworking of the parable by the early church. This reaction against the presence of allegory in the parables of Jesus is explained primarily by the fact that Jülicher depended on Aristotle and Greek theories of rhetoric[1] for defining what a parable is rather than upon the Old Testament. Through the work of such men as Christian August Bugge[2] and especially Paul Fiebig,[3] however, it became clear that Jülicher had not only turned Jesus into an educated nineteenth-century German liberal theologian, but that he also had him educated according to classical Greek learning rather than in the environment of first-century Judaism. Fiebig pointed out in his study of the rabbinic parables that many of them contained allegorical details. He then concluded, "I would characterize the Jewish similitudes (*Gleichnisse*) as 'Parables (*Parabeln*)' with a mixture of allegory."[4] It is furthermore now evident that Jesus, as well as Paul, should be understood in the context of the Old Testament and first-century Judaism rather than in the context of the Greek classical writers. As has been pointed out above,[5] not all Old Testament and rabbinic parables are similitudes, for the term *mashal* can refer to a proverb, a taunt, a riddle, a story parable, or even an allegory. One cannot, therefore, say *a priori* that a parable cannot contain any allegorical elements or that Jesus could not have included allegorical elements in his parables.[6] Whether the parables of Jesus at times contain allegorical details and whether these details are authentic must be demonstrated on exegetical grounds, not on classical Greek philological or *a priori* philosophical presuppositions. Nevertheless, it would appear to be a wise rule not to interpret the parables of Jesus or the details of the parables allegorically[7] unless such an interpretation is absolutely necessary. We should find allegory in the parables of Jesus only when we must, not simply when we can!

The second weakness of Jülicher's work was that the one main point that he saw in the parables of Jesus was always a general moral truth. Jülicher was a liberal who wrote during the reign of liberal theology. It was therefore natural for him to see in the one point of the parables a general tenet of nineteenth-century liberalism. One example of this is his treatment of the parable of the prodigal son (Luke 15:11-32), to which he devotes more space than any other. In this parable the *tertium comparationis* is seen as "an elevated revelation over a fundamental question of religion, namely, 'Dare the God of righteousness accept sinners in grace?' " (II, 363). A second example is found in the parable of the unjust steward (Luke 16:1-8), where the one main point of comparison is the generalization that "determined use of the present is a prerequisite for a happy future" (II, 511). Still another example is found in the parable of the talents (Matt 25:14-30), which has as its one main point of comparison the principle that "reward is only earned by performance" (II, 485).[8] It is not surprising, therefore, to see Jesus described by Jülicher in true liberal fashion as an "apostle of progress" (II, 483) who taught in each parable a moral law which was intended to rule the hearts and minds of men. Yet unlike the liberal Jesus of Jülicher

who uttered general moral truths, the Jesus of the parables so
disturbed and enraged some of his listeners that they sought to destroy
him (MARK 12:12; 14:1-2). They would never have bothered to do this
if all he did was to teach the general moral truths of theological
liberalism. Yet despite these two limitations, the world of biblical
scholarship will be forever indebted to Jülicher for having broken once
and for all the stranglehold that the allegorical method of interpretation
held on the interpretation of the parables. Using the insight of Jülicher,
we can formulate our FIRST PRINCIPLE for the investigation of the parables
as follows:

> I. SEEK THE ONE MAIN POINT OF THE PARABLE. DO NOT
> SEEK ALLEGORICAL SIGNIFICANCE IN THE DETAILS OF
> A PARABLE UNLESS IT IS ABSOLUTELY NECESSARY.[9]

Ascertaining the main point that Jesus intended is not as easy as it
may at first appear. Some general questions that are helpful are:

1. What was the general theological framework out of which Jesus
taught?

2. What were some of the possible audiences to which Jesus
addressed his parables? Does the parable being investigated fit any of
these audiences especially well?

3. What possible or hoped-for response was Jesus seeking by his use
of the parable?

4. What was the political/religious/economic environment of Palestine when Jesus spoke the parable?

In addition to these general questions, some specific questions that
should be asked are:

1. What terms are repeated in the parable? Which are not?

2. Upon what does the parable dwell, i.e., to what or to whom does
the parable devote the most space?

3. What is the main contrast found in the parable?

4. What comes at the end of the parable? (This has been called "the
rule of end stress.")

5. What is spoken in direct discourse in the parable? (Frequently
what is most important in the parable appears in direct discourse.)

6. What characters appear in the parable? Which are the least
important? Which are the two most important characters? (Usually a
parable zeroes in on two characters to establish its main point.)

7. How would you have told the parable? If Jesus told it differently,
does this reveal anything?

The value and importance of this principle become clear when we seek to interpret certain parables such as the parable of the hidden treasure (Matt 13:44): "The kingdom of heaven is like treasure hidden in a field, which a man found and covered up; then in his joy he goes and sells all that he has and buys that field." In investigating this parable we must remember Jülicher's contribution to the study of the parables. We should not press the details of the parable for allegorical significance but should seek rather to ascertain the one main point that the parable is making. To concern ourselves, therefore, over the morality, or better yet the immorality (the man in the parable is certainly not following the Golden Rule!), of the man in the parable is to miss the point. Jesus is not advocating such immoral or amoral behavior, for the deception involved clearly violates the Golden Rule (MATT 7:12). The behavior of the man in the parable simply provides the local coloring for the story. Perhaps there had recently taken place just such an incident which Jesus now used to provide interest and flavor to his parable. The one main point that Jesus is seeking to make in the parable is clear. It is worth the surrender of everything to enter the kingdom of God! The parable of the great pearl (Matt 13:45-46) makes this very same point and was no doubt placed alongside this parable for this reason, but here the behavior of the merchant is clearly moral.[10]

Two other parables in which the issue of morality, if raised, can confuse the interpreter are the parable of the wise and foolish virgins (Matt 25:1-13) and the parable of the unjust steward (Luke 16:1-8). In the former, the five maidens, whom the audience is told to emulate because they are wise, are in a sense quite selfish in not sharing their oil, and this writer can still remember a leading American churchman preaching from this text and concluding that Christians should not be like those five virgins who had oil and refused to share it! If he had been aware of our first principle for interpreting the parables, he would not have pressed such details and would have simply accepted them as local coloring which was meant to add interest to the story. The one main point is clear. Be ready at all times, for you do not know when the consummation will take place! (If one interprets this parable along the lines of "realized" eschatology, the main point may vary somewhat, *but* it will still remain true that one should not press the detail that the wise virgins appear selfish and "unchristian.") In the parable of the unjust steward we have a similar dilemma in that the commended steward (Luke 16:8) is both a scoundrel and a thief. He is not commended, however, for his thievery but for his wisdom, for, having seen the coming judgment (Luke 16:2), he wisely prepared himself for it. John Calvin's treatment of this parable deserves to be quoted at length.

> Here, too, we can easily see how foolish it would be to insist on the details. There is nothing laudable in giving away other men's goods; and who would put up with a dishonest rascal robbing him and letting off his debtors at will? It would be too crass altogether for a man to see part of his possessions embezzled and the rest given away by the thief, and then approve of it. But all Christ meant was, as He adds just after, that heathen and worldly men are more industrious and clever in taking care of the ways and means of this fleeting world than God's children are in caring for the heavenly and eternal life, or making it their study and exercise.[11]

The one main point of the parable involves prudent behavior in the light of a coming judgment. Jesus came preaching, "The time is fulfilled, and the kingdom of God is at hand; repent, and believe in the gospel" (MARK 1:15). Jesus' audience therefore stands at a point of crisis. The kingdom of God has dawned, and with it has come the turning point of history. One must decide and that decision will determine eternity! The one main point of the parable is that, seeing this crisis and impending judgment, one must be wise and prepare for it. The parable tells its hearers, "Be wise, for judgment is at hand! Prepare!" How does one prepare for this crisis? Certainly Jesus does not intend that his listeners assume that he is urging them to be wise thieves! Rather, a specific application is given in v. 9, either by Jesus or by the Evangelist, which involves the wise use of money.[12]

By applying our first principle to the interpretation of the parables, we shall keep ourselves from making the mistake of concentrating on the details of the parables rather than on their main point.[13]

C. H. DODD—JOACHIM JEREMIAS

It was C. H. Dodd who, more than anyone else, contributed the second major insight and principle to the investigation of the parables. It is true that others, such as W. H. Robinson[14] and A. T. Cadoux,[15] had earlier drawn attention to the fact that the parables should be interpreted in their original context and setting, but it was C. H. Dodd more than anyone else who brought about, in his *The Parables of the Kingdom* (1936), the next major advance in parabolic interpretation after

Jülicher. Dodd pointed out that to understand the parables properly we should recognize that Jesus did not address them to a nineteenth- or twentieth-century audience but, on the contrary, to the men and women of the first century who listened to him. This point is so self-evident that at first glance it appears unnecessary even to mention it, but the consequences that flow out from this understanding are extremely important. Up to the time of Dodd the investigation of the parables was so concerned with the significance of the parables for their readers that they were interpreted primarily in the context of the present situation and time of each reader. It was Dodd, who, more than anyone else, pointed out that to understand the parables correctly one needed to interpret them first of all in their original *Sitz im Leben*, i.e., in their original setting in the life of Jesus and in the context of his ministry. In other words, before one should seek to understand the significance of the parables for one's own situation today, one should seek the original meaning of the parables and their application for Jesus' audience in the first century. If we were to reword this in still another way, we could say that Dodd demonstrated that the question, What is the meaning of this parable for me/us today? must be preceded by the question, What did the parable mean when it was uttered by Jesus during his ministry?

Building upon the work of the early form critics, Dodd realized that the present location of the parables in the Gospels was frequently due to logical and theological considerations rather than chronological ones. As a result, at times one may not be able to ascertain the exact location in the life of Jesus in which a particular parable was uttered. In such instances Dodd, however, argued that one should then seek to understand

(i) such ideas as may be supposed to have been in the minds of the hearers of Jesus during his ministry [and]
(ii) the general orientation of the teaching of Jesus.[16]

Dodd then proceeded to apply this insight to the investigation of the parables, and the results were impressive. It became evident that the parables, removed from the blinders of the present, were not simply altruistic general analogies of eternal truths but often weapons of controversy by which Jesus sought to break down the prejudices and standards of his audience. At times they were damning indictments of his opponents' views and values; at times they were powerful counterarguments; at times they were a brilliant defense of his actions! Clearly Dodd is correct, for it is extremely important to understand what Jesus assumed in the knowledge, experience, and attitude of his listeners as well as to have a general idea of the main tenor of his teaching, for when this is done, the parables breathe a new life and excitement.

It should not be assumed, however, that Dodd's work is not without its own limitations, for his own understanding of the nature of Jesus' eschatological teachings was frequently read into the text and caused him to interpret some of the parables quite artificially. Dodd believed that the message of Jesus consisted of only a "realized" eschatological dimension. According to this view the kingdom of God was, according to Jesus, an entirely present phenomenon. In his coming the kingdom of God had come in its entirety. In contrast to "consistent" eschatology, which argued that Jesus understood the kingdom of God to be an entirely future event even though that future was very near, Dodd believed that Jesus taught that the kingdom of God had come in its completeness in his own ministry. There was nothing still unfulfilled or incomplete. The kingdom of God had come in its entirety in the ministry of Jesus! As a result of this conviction Dodd interpreted all the parables from the viewpoint of "realized" eschatology. For Dodd, even such eschatological parables as MARK 13:28-30 (the fig tree); MATT 24:45-51 (the wise and foolish servants); Matt 25:1-13 (the wise and foolish virgins); Luke 12:35-38 (the watchful servants); etc., refer not to a future eschatological judgment but to a situation and crisis in the earthly ministry of Jesus. Such traditional eschatological symbolism, according to Dodd, was used by Jesus simply to indicate the otherworldly and absolute character of the kingdom of God which had now come in its completeness in Jesus' ministry. As a result, "it seems possible, therefore, to give to all these 'eschatological' parables an application within the context of the ministry of Jesus."[17] It is evident today that Dodd's interpretation of the eschatological teachings of Jesus is only partially correct. Jesus did not teach either a purely "realized" eschatology or a purely "consistent" eschatology. Rather, he taught both! For Jesus, the kingdom of God had both come in the fulfillment of the Old Testament promises and was at the same time a future reality that awaited consummation.[18]

The importance of Dodd's contribution to the study of the parables cannot be overstated. Joachim Jeremias, whose work *Die Gleichnisse Jesu* (1947 and subsequent editions) is still probably the most valuable single reference for the interpretation of the parables available today, states:

How much the work is indebted for stimulus and instruction to C. H. Dodd's fundamentally important book *The Parables of the Kingdom*, London, 1936, is indicated at many points. Professor Dodd's book has opened a new era in the study of the parables; although differences of opinion with regard to some details may exist, yet it is unthinkable that there should ever be any retreat from the essential lines laid down by Dodd for the interpretation of the parables of Jesus.[19]

Yet what Dodd did in a preliminary way, Jeremias carried out systematically and in detail. For this Jeremias was eminently qualified, for he has demonstrated his mastery of the environment and religious customs of Jesus' day[20] as well as the mother tongue of Jesus. When one adds to this demonstrated expertise his view that the call of God is to be found exclusively in the life, acts, and words of Jesus and that all else found in the New Testament canon is at best a response or witness to this divine call, it is not surprising to find that it is Jeremias more than any other scholar who has sought to ascertain the *ipsissima verba*, or actual words, of Jesus in the parables.[21] There is, therefore, no better work available as a source for understanding the context of the *Sitz im Leben* of Jesus. We can summarize the contribution of Dodd and Jeremias, which is our SECOND PRINCIPLE for interpreting the parables, as follows:

II. SEEK TO UNDERSTAND THE *SITZ IM LEBEN* IN WHICH THE PARABLE WAS UTTERED.

Two parables that take on new meaning and excitement when interpreted in the light of the ministry of Jesus and his situation are the parables of the lost sheep and the lost coin.

What man of you, having a hundred sheep, if he has lost one of them, does not leave the ninety-nine in the wilderness, and go after the one which is lost, until he finds it? And when he has found it, he lays it on his shoulders, rejoicing. And when he comes home, he calls together his friends and his neighbors, saying to them, "Rejoice with me, for I have found my sheep which was lost." Just so, I tell you, there will be more joy in heaven over one sinner who repents than over ninety-nine righteous persons who need no repentance. (LUKE 15:4-7)

Or what woman, having ten silver coins, if she loses one coin, does not light a lamp and sweep the house and seek diligently until she finds it? And when she has found it, she calls together her friends and neighbors, saying, "Rejoice with me, for I have found the coin which I had lost." Just so, I tell you, there is joy before the angels of God over one sinner who repents. (Luke 15:8-10)

Generally, the two parables above and the longer parable of the gracious father that follows are seen as beautiful examples of the love of God for sinners, and of course they are. We gain additional insight into these parables, however, if we seek to understand them in the context or *Sitz im Leben* of the historical Jesus. To be sure, Jesus meant these parables to be examples of the divine love for the lost, but we must also seek to understand the particular situation in which they were spoken. Most scholars agree that the context into which Luke places these parables is a correct one. These parables were spoken to the Pharisees and scribes who were protesting the conduct of Jesus in eating with publicans and sinners (Luke 15:1-2). That this was not an isolated incident is evident from such passages as MARK 2:16-17; MATT 11:19; Luke 7:39; 19:7. These three parables were therefore uttered as an apology against such criticism. But what is the significance of "this man receiving sinners and eating with them"? The significance of this act is that in the ministry of Jesus, God was at work now seeking the lost sheep of Israel! This same point is made in each of the three parables in Luke 15. Understood in the context of the first *Sitz im Leben*, these parables are more than just simply examples of God's redeeming love. They are both an apology and a proclamation. They are an apology or defense of Jesus' behavior in associating with publicans, sinners, and harlots, and they are a proclamation that in this activity God is now visiting his people in fulfillment of the Old Testament promises. The eschatological significance is clear. The kingdom of God has come! God is now visiting the rejected of Israel (cf. MATT 11:4-6 with Isa 35:5-6; 61:1)! In the ministry of Jesus, God is fulfilling the Old Testament promises and now visiting the lost sheep of Israel.

REDACTION CRITICISM

With the rise of redaction criticism, still another insight has been gained as to how to interpret the parables. Since the work of Hans Conzelmann[22] and Willi Marxsen[23] in the mid-fifties, there has resulted a great interest in the theological emphases and interpretations that the Evangelists gave to the materials which they incorporated into their Gospels. It is now evident that the Gospel writers were not simply scissors-and-paste editors who glued and pasted various traditions together but rather theologians who interpreted these traditions to meet the needs of their audience. As a result, it is important to understand and interpret the parables in the light of the third *Sitz im Leben*, i.e., the life situation of the Evangelists.[24] Since at times a parable that originally was directed to a hostile audience such as the Pharisees and the scribes in the first *Sitz im Leben* is now directed in the third *Sitz im Leben* to the church, it is important to investigate how the Evangelists interpreted and applied the parables to their own situations. This will not only enlighten us as to the situation of the Evangelist and what he was seeking to accomplish in the writing of his Gospel but will also help us later on when we seek to apply these parables to our own situation in life today.

The reader may have noted at this point that nothing has been said about interpreting the parables in the context of the second *Sitz im Leben*, i.e., during the oral period when the parables were circulating by word of mouth. The present writer is, of course, aware of the possibility of doing this and the value that such an investigation has in shedding light on a "history of tradition" understanding of how the parables were interepreted. He is even more aware that any attempt to understand the *Sitz im Leben* in which the parables were uttered (principle II) and how the Evangelists interpreted the parables (principle III) requires that one investigate how the parables were interpreted during the second *Sitz im Leben*. He has not dealt with this in the book primarily for two reasons. The first reason is that, whereas he attributes divine authority to both the words of Jesus and the writings of the Evangelists, he does not believe that the same authority can be attributed to the different interpretations of parables by the church during the oral period. As a result, although it is necessary to investigate how the parables were interpreted during the oral period, such an investigation serves primarily as a means by which we can ascertain the dominical and the Evangelists' interpretations of the parables, for these possess a unique and divine authority. The second reason is that, whereas we possess the writings and, as a result, the final interpretation of the Evangelists and can compare their actual words with the presumed words of Jesus, in seeking to investigate the second *Sitz im Leben*, one must deal with the presumed words of Jesus as well as the presumed interpretation of those words by the early church. This is much more difficult because we are comparing two hypothetical reconstructions with each other rather than one such reconstruction (the *ipsissima verba* or *vox* of Jesus) with a given (the final interpretation of the Evangelists).

As a result of the contribution of redaction criticism to the study of the Gospels, we can arrive at our THIRD PRINCIPLE for interpreting the parables.

III. SEEK TO UNDERSTAND HOW THE EVANGELIST INTERPRETED
THE PARABLE.

An example of how this principle applies can be shown in the investigation of the parable of the pounds.

> He said therefore, "A nobleman went into a far country to receive a kingdom and then return. Calling ten of his servants, he gave them ten pounds, and said to them, 'Trade with these till I come.' But his citizens hated him and sent an embassy after him, saying, 'We do not want this man to reign over us.' When he returned, having received the kingdom, he commanded these servants, to whom he had given the money, to be called to him, that he might know what they had gained by trading. The first came before him, saying, 'Lord, your pound has made ten pounds more.' And he said to him, 'Well done, good servant! Because you have been faithful in a very little, you shall have authority over ten cities.' And the second came, saying, 'Lord, your pound has made five pounds.' And he said to him, 'And you are to be over five cities.' Then another came, saying, 'Lord, here is your pound, which I kept laid away in a napkin; for I was afraid of you, because you are a severe man; you take up what you did not lay down, and reap what you did not sow.' He said to him 'I will condemn you out of your own mouth, you wicked servant! You knew that I was a severe man, taking up what I did not lay down and reaping what I did not sow? Why then did you not put my money into the bank, and at my coming I should have collected it with interest?' And he said to those who stood by, 'Take the pound from him, and give it to him who has ten pounds.' (And they said to him, 'Lord, he has ten pounds!') 'I tell you, that to every one who has will more be given; but from him who has not, even what he has will be taken away. But as for these enemies of mine, who did not want me to reign over them, bring them here and slay them before me.' " (Luke 19:12-27)

For our purpose it is not important to discuss which of the elements of the parable may have been added during the oral period or to note the total redaction of the Evangelist with regard to the parable and its implications. Rather, we shall simply note one unique understanding which the Evangelist gave to this parable because of a need present in his situation in the third *Sitz im Leben*. Most scholars today see in Luke's Gospel a concern by the author over a problem that disturbed many Christians in the early church. The problem involved the delay of the parousia (cf. 2 Peter 3:3f.). Luke in his use of this parable directed himself to this problem. He does so by reassuring his reader(s) that such a delay was in keeping with the very teachings of Jesus, for he taught that there would be just such a delay. In fact, Jesus taught this very parable of the pounds because his disciples "supposed that the kingdom of God was to appear immediately" (Luke 19:11). Luke seeks to point out through this parable and his redaction of this parable that Jesus himself taught that he would be away for a period of time and that during this period his disciples should concern themselves with being faithful stewards. In the Lukan setting this parable of "stewardship" is given a particular emphasis by the Evangelist that is meaningful for his own situation. That such an emphasis by Luke is not contrary to the original meaning of the parable is evident for two reasons. For one, the whole principle of stewardship has meaning only if there is a period of time between the "present" and the consummation, i.e., the stewardship which Jesus taught in the parable implies—no, rather necessitates—a delay of some sort between the time of Jesus and the final consummation. The teaching of faithful stewardship only has meaning if there is a period of time before the consummation for practicing stewardship. Luke therefore points out that by telling this parable Jesus himself revealed that there would be a period of time before the consummation, i.e., that there would be a delay in the parousia! Secondly, the Matthean version of the parable also contains this emphasis on the delay of the master's return, for we read in Matt 25:19, "Now *after a long time* the master . . . came and settled accounts" (italics added). Therefore, whereas the main point of the parable for Jesus may lie in the area of faithful stewardship, Luke is not misinterpreting it by his treatment of the parable but rather is emphasizing for his own particular situation that this implies a delay in the consummation.

RECENT DISCUSSION ON THE PARABLES

Recent discussion involving the parables has centered around the application to parable research of two different disciplines: structural analysis[25] and aesthetic criticism.[26] The former concerns itself primarily with the "deep structures" of meaning which lie below the surface of a narrative. Believing that this deep structure is expressed in common codes of kinship patterns that operate in the author's mind at an unconscious level, they seek to identify the meaningful units of a text and arrive at the deeper structure and meaning of the text. Aesthetic criticism, in contrast to structuralism, is more concerned with the larger units and the surface level of a text and seeks to understand the text in the light of such literary forms and paradigms as tragedy, comedy, etc.[27] Borrowing a great deal from the recent linguistic analysis of analogy, simile, and metaphor, the parables are seen as aesthetic objects or timeless artistic creations which possess a vitality and power in and of themselves.[28] With these two new approaches a whole new vocabulary has arisen, and we now come across in the discussion of the parables such terms as language event, polyvalence, plurisignificant, comic parable, metaparable, tragic parable, autonomous, autotelic, mimetic and ludic allegory, trope.

By far the more frequently used new approach is aesthetic criticism. Here a great deal of emphasis is placed upon the difference between simile and metaphor. This difference is seen not so much in the area of pure form, i.e., a simile is an explicit comparison using such terms as "like" or "as" while a metaphor is an implied comparison, but in the area of the existential quality of these forms. A simile is seen as being basically illustrative in nature whereas a metaphor is seen as being creative of meaning.[29] A metaphor is therefore more than a sign that illustrates a certain reality. On the contrary, a metaphor is a bearer of that very reality to which it refers. According to this literary approach, the parables, simply because of their metaphorical nature, are believed to contain a power or force within them independent of any historical context.[30] As a result, the parables are able to mediate directly to their hearers the reality of the "language event" contained within them not because they are parables of Jesus but simply because they are parables. The very fact that the parables use the literary quality of metaphor indicates that they are not the kind of speech that conveys information to the hearer, i.e., they do not seek to add content to the reservoir of the hearer's knowledge, but rather parables seek because of their literary form to affect the hearer's attitude and compel from him a decision. Since the parable possesses this power to shape and change such attitudes, a parable is not simply a literary form conveying information but rather a language event, and as a language event it introduces its readers to a new possiblity of existence by calling them into judgment and decision.

Parables, like all aesthetic works, are also seen as "autonomous" or "autotelic." They are, in other words, independent of the intention of their authors (this would be the so-called "intentional fallacy") or the effects that such a parable had or has on its hearers (this would be the so-called "affective fallacy"). On the contrary, a parable, because of its aesthetic and autotelic nature must be considered an end in itself and carries within itself its own purpose.[31] Only if we view the parables as autonomous-autotelic aesthetic works of art can their living quality be preserved, for if we follow the views of Dodd and Jeremias, we shall chain the parables to the first century, and thus they will become nothing more than "archaeological" artifacts of the past rather than language events of the twentieth century capable of transforming their present-day readers by offering to them the possibility of a new authentic existence. Rather than thinking a la Dodd and Jeremias that we can interpret the parable, we should acknowledge that the parable, because of its literary form, possesses an innate power that can and should interpret us.[32]

When this understanding is applied to the New Testament parables, this means that the parables are not to be understood as vehicles which Jesus used to teach certain truths about the kingdom of God or about God himself. They do not convey meaning or content about the kingdom of God. Rather, they are to be understood as engaging their hearers and compelling them to participate in an existential experience (language event) bringing them to judgment and decision. Through these parables the readers/listeners enter into and participate in the very reality of the kingdom of God. As a result, the parables are not to be interpreted by their hearers but rather are to interpret *them* and confront them with the need of understanding themselves in the light of the judgment and grace of God. In reading the parables of Jesus we should therefore realize that these parables do not function as objects to be studied and analyzed but are open-ended realities that encounter us and bring us to the place of decision. As one writer has said, "The Kingdom comes to expression in parable as parable; the parables of Jesus bring the Reign of God to expression as parable."[33]

Intimately associated with this approach to the parables is the view that the parables are not limited to a single meaning or point as Jülicher, Dodd, and Jeremias maintain. They are, on the contrary, "polyvalent" or "polysignificant." Since the way in which parables became language events is different for each hearer or reader, the meaning of the same parable will of necessity also be different for each individual. The open-ended nature of the parables requires, therefore, that they be acknowledged as polyvalent and not limited to a single meaning.

It is clear from the above that this literary-aesthetic interpretation of the parables as language event has grasped an important truth. Jesus' parables are not meant simply to supply data to be stored in some theological data bank. On the contrary, they are vehicles meant to bring decision. Yet there are some serious criticisms of this view that must be mentioned. For one, when Jesus said after the parable of the sower and the soils, "'He who has ears to hear, let him hear'" (MARK 4:9), it is difficult to assume that what he meant was, "Let anyone find whatever meaning is contained in this literary form" or "Let the hearers be interpreted by this metaphor as they will." It seems far more reasonable to assume that what Jesus meant was, "Listen to what I am saying through this parable!"[34] This view is supported by the following Markan summary.

> With many such parables he spoke the word to them, as they were able to hear it; he did not speak to them without a parable, but privately to his own disciples he explained everything. (MARK 4:33-34)

For Mark the parables were clearly a means Jesus used to teach "the word," i.e., his message.[35] Furthermore, the very fact that Jesus explained his parables to his disciples (MARK 4:33-34; 7:14-22) indicates that they were not considered by Jesus (or at least by the Evangelist)[36] as autotelic or as Rorschach tests which hearers could interpret (or be interpreted by) as they thought best.[37] Rather, what was paramount was what Jesus meant to teach by the parables, i.e., the message Jesus placed in the parables. It is also difficult for this writer to assume that when Jesus explained a parable he at the same time gave different and varied interpretations. One receives the impression from the Gospels that when Jesus explained a parable he taught the meaning of the parable which he intended, so that at least in the first *Sitz im Leben* the parables were seen to reveal a specific "word" of Jesus rather than several different "words" contained autonomously in the parable itself. What Raymond E. Brown has said about hermeneutics in general can also be said about the parables.

> Our judgment on this is that no text of Scripture can have two heterogeneous, independent literal senses, for quite obviously no author [or speaker] intends to have his words convey two totally unrelated meanings.[38]

Secondly, throughout the centuries Christians have read, studied, and delighted themselves in the parables of Jesus precisely because they were just that—parables *of Jesus*. They are not anonymous *ex nihilo* literary creations. They came into being at a point of time from the very mind of Jesus. As a result, a Christological issue comes into play. Whereas the early church attributed to Jesus deity and thus a divine authority, and whereas the early church attributed to the writing of the Evangelists a divine inspiration and thus a divine authority as well, it seems that recent literary criticism of the parables has attributed deity to the parabolic form itself. The power to challenge and transform is seen to lie in the metaphorical power of the parable itself. Using the terminology of systematic theology, we find that some literary critics have attributed the power of "regeneration" to a literary form rather than to God himself. The authority of the parables and its ability to transform lives, however, comes not from magical power residing in the literary form of metaphor, but on the contrary it comes from the authority of the "Parabler" and the truth contained in his parables!

A final criticism that can be leveled at this approach to the parables is that it loses sight of the historical context in which the parables were uttered. To speak of the intrinsic power and force of the parables and their "open-endedness," i.e., that their meaning is not determined by the original intent of Jesus, may be in vogue today, but ultimately such treatment of the parables will only lead to misinterpretation and confusion.[39] It should be remembered that the allegorical method of interpreting the parables saw in the parables a kind of open-endedness! The loss or neglect of the historical context, i.e., the nonapplication of our second principle for interpreting the parables, has led to all sorts of abuse of the text by means of allegorizing, and it is not surprising that some of the more recent literary-critical treatments of the parables make one think that Origen has been raised from the dead as a twentieth-century existentialist. Only by attempting to understand the parables in their original *Sitz im Leben* shall we be able to free ourselves from the chains of modern-day fads or trends, whether they be liberalism's general moral truth or existentialism's language event.[40] The greatest reverence we can give to the parables of Jesus is not to treat them as literary accounts that are ends in themselves but rather to treat them as the parables *of Jesus*, i.e., as parables Jesus taught and which are filled with his meaning and insight! What he means today by his parables cannot be treated apart from the question of what he meant by them in the first *Sitz im Leben*.

Although the present author has serious reservations concerning the more recent discussion of the parables, he does agree that a purely historical-critical analysis of the parables according to the first three principles of parable interpretation given above, if it ends at this point, "profiteth little"! Apart from the application of the message of the parables to one's own life, such investigation is a futile exercise in historical research or textual archaeology. The parables were/are the Word of God. They are therefore able to speak to us today. As a result, we can formulate our FOURTH AND FINAL PRINCIPLE for the interpretation of the parables as follows:

IV. SEEK WHAT GOD IS SAYING TO US TODAY THROUGH THE PARABLE.

Unless the reader of the parables comes to this point, the study of the parables is of little real value, for what does it profit a person to gain all sorts of historical understanding of the parables and yet lose their significance for today? It must be pointed out, however, that the fourth principle of parabolic interpretation is not independent or isolated from the first three principles. On the contrary, apart from the application of the first three principles there is little hope for an accurate application of the last principle. The true understanding of the one main point (principle I) intended by Jesus (principle II) and the understanding of the Evangelists (principle III) are to serve as the framework in which we understand what God is saying to us today as we read the parables (principle IV). Although the particular understanding of what God is saying to us through a particular parable may vary from what he is saying to someone else, our interpretation of a parable, as well as anyone else's, must be in harmony and in continuity with its interpretation in the first and the third *Sitz im Leben*.

Another way of saying this is that whereas there is usually a single meaning of a parable in the first and the third *Sitz im Leben*, since no author or speaker intends his words to have two totally different meanings, the significance of that meaning may be different for the present-day reader. The significance, although different for different readers, must nevertheless stay within the limits of the intention of Jesus and the Evangelists.

Unless the first three principles form the framework in which our understanding of what the parable is saying to us is shaped, the interpretation of the parables will tend to degenerate into a completely subjective experience in which our feelings (whether liberal, evangelical, or existential) have become the absolute and final authority, i.e., our feelings have become God's final revelation! Surely it is far better to seek by the historical investigation of the parable to arrive, if possible, at what the text originally meant in the first and the third *Sitz im Leben* and then to allow the Spirit of God to use this understanding to speak to our own situation. It is only then that the parables will truly become to us the living Word of God. It should be pointed out, however, that those who believe that the parables will then simply confirm their present religious life-style and beliefs and bring them assurance and comfort are destined for a surprise! Properly understood, the parables will be as demanding, threatening, rebuking, as well as encouraging and promising, to us as they were to Jesus' hearers.

CHAPTER 6

INTERPRETING THE PARABLES TODAY

THE FOUR BASIC PRINCIPLES for interpreting the parables will now be applied to a particular parable. We shall apply these principles in the order in which they were discussed in the previous chapter. It must be acknowledged, however, that our investigation will, of necessity, possess a certain amount of circular reasoning in that one cannot seek to ascertain the one main point of the parable apart from seeking to interpret the parable in its original *Sitz im Leben*, and one cannot do this without understanding how the Evangelist has interpreted the parable in the third *Sitz im Leben*. There is also a sense in which it may be more correct to proceed backward from principle III to principles II and I, and in practice this may often be the way one investigates a parable, but we shall proceed along the lines of the historical development of interpretation as outlined in the previous chapter. In so doing we hope that the lessons learned in the past from Jülicher, Dodd, and the redaction critics will as a result continually be reinforced. Since we have dealt at greater length in the previous chapter with the parable of the good Samaritan than with any other parable, we shall use this parable as an example of how to interpret the parables of Jesus.

I. SEEK THE ONE MAIN POINT OF THE PARABLE.

In its present context it is clear that the allegorical interpretation of this parable is incorrect. Far from charting a *heilsgeschichtlich* scheme of redemption or advancing a Christological portrayal of Jesus, the parable both in its introduction and its conclusion indicates that the main point of its teaching involves the question of "Who is my neighbor?" or "Who proved to be the neighbor?" The parable is connected to Jesus' teaching concerning the great commandment (Luke 10:25-28) and is introduced as follows:

> But he, desiring to justify himself, said to Jesus, "And who is my neighbor?" (Luke 10:29)

and it concludes with:

> "Which of these three, do you think, proved neighbor to the man who fell among robbers?" He said, "The one who showed mercy on him." (Luke 10:36-37a)

It is clear, therefore, that in its present context the main point of the parable centers around the question of who is a neighbor or what it means to be a neighbor.

While it is admitted today by almost all scholars that in its present context the parable of the good Samaritan seeks to answer the question "Who is my neighbor?" many scholars argue that the present context is not original and therefore cannot be used to interpret the original meaning of the parable. It is also frequently argued that Luke 10:25-29 and 10:37 could not have been joined to the parable originally for the following reasons: (1) Since Luke 10:25-29 is a parallel to MARK 12:28-31 and MATT 22:34-40 and since neither Mark nor Matthew contains the parable, the insertion of the parable of the good Samaritan into the context of the pericope of the greatest commandment is due to Luke and is therefore secondary. (2) There is a logical inconsistency between the meaning of "neighbor" in Luke 10:27,29 and in Luke 10:36, for in the two former passages the neighbor is the object of love, i.e., he is the one who is to be loved, whereas in the latter passage he is the subject of love, i.e., he is the one who is doing the loving.

These objections have been attacked from a number of directions. Jeremias, along with T. W. Manson and others, has argued that LUKE 10:25-28 is not simply a parallel to MARK 12:28-34, for the only thing these passages have in common is the double command to love, and "it is quite probable that Jesus often uttered so important a thought as that contained in the double command,"[1] for "great teachers constantly repeat themselves."[2] Concerning the difference between the meaning of the word "neighbor" in Luke 10:27,29 and Luke 10:36, Jeremias argues:

> It is simply a formal inconsistency in which there is nothing surprising when once the philological facts are realized: the word *rea'* implies a reciprocal relation, like our word "comrade."[3]

Despite what Jeremias says, however, it does appear that there is a difference in the use of the term "neighbor" by the scribe and by Jesus that must not be overlooked, but it is the very kind of difference which one might expect to come from the lips of Jesus. Rather than seeing here a conflict between the parable and the pericope of the great commandment, we should see here a conflict between the lawyer's concept of "what it means to be my neighbor" and Jesus' concept of "what it means for me to be a neighbor." Elsewhere in a similar manner Jesus demonstrates that the actions of his followers are not to be in any way dependent upon any quality in the object of love.[4] We are not to concern ourselves, as the lawyer apparently was doing, with what a person must do to qualify as an object of our love. We are to concern ourselves only with loving. In his very question the lawyer revealed his basic misconception of the great commandment. Whereas he was concerned with who qualified as a recipient of his love, Jesus' understanding of the great commandment was to be concerned with qualifying as a lover! In Luke, Jesus states:

> Love your enemies, do good to those who hate you, bless those who curse you, pray for those who abuse you. (LUKE 6:27-28)

Love is not dependent upon the object of love being able to qualify and meet certain requirements. The issue is not "Who is to be loved?", i.e., "Who is my neighbor?", but rather "What does it mean for me to love?", i.e., "What does it mean for me to be a neighbor?" Thus Jesus tells us to

> lend, expecting nothing in return; and your reward will be great, and you will be sons of the Most High; for he is kind to the ungrateful and the selfish. Be merciful, even as your Father is merciful. (LUKE 6:35-36)

Our lending is to be totally independent of the ability to repay! In fact, we should lend especially to those who cannot repay (Luke 6:34). We are likewise to invite to our banquet those who cannot repay us with a return invitation (Luke 14:12-14). All this indicates that the twist we find in Jesus' use of the term "neighbor" is fully in accord with his teachings elsewhere. Whereas Judaism and the lawyer were concerned with the question "What must a person do or be to qualify as my neighbor?", Jesus clearly rebukes this question with the parable and demonstrates that our concern is to be a loving neighbor! Far from seeing, therefore, a logical inconsistency in the use of the term "neighbor" and concluding as a result that Luke 10:25-37 originally existed as two independent traditions, we should note that this logical inconsistency exists because of the misconception of Jesus' contemporaries. The manner in which Jesus in Luke 10:25-37 rebuked this misconception is, however, perfectly consistent with his teachings elsewhere and argues strongly for the unity of the passage.[5]

Even if it is not possible to demonstrate the unity of Luke 10:25-37, however, it would appear that Luke 10:29 belongs to the parable and is not simply a Lukan editorial seam for the following reasons: (1) The way Luke 10:36 is worded seems to assume that the term "neighbor" has already been mentioned, and apart from Luke 10:29 (and Luke 10:27) this term is not found in the account. (2) Luke would not have needed to create verse 29 to link the parable to Luke 10:25-28. All he would have needed would have been "And he told them this parable" (cf. Luke 15:3), and something like this, according to this theory, must have already introduced the parable. (3) Whereas the question "Who is my neighbor?" was an important and much debated issue in the Judaism of Jesus' day, it is less easy to discover a *Sitz im Leben* in the early church where this was a debated issue.[6]

It would appear, then, that from the very beginning the parable of the good Samaritan was associated with the question of "Who is (or what does it mean to be) a neighbor?" As a result, in seeking the one main point of this parable, we should seek to find that one main point in the answer to this question!

II. SEEK TO UNDERSTAND THE *SITZ IM LEBEN* IN WHICH THE PARABLE WAS UTTERED.

One of the difficulties involved in seeking to understand the meaning of this parable in the first *Sitz im Leben* is that the various terms used in the parable evoke attitudes and responses in the reader today which are quite different from and even antithetical to those evoked in the hearers in Jesus' day. The very term "Samaritan" is an excellent example of this. The present writer still remembers playing a game with his daughter, who was eleven or twelve at the time, in which he asked her to tell him the first words that came into her mind at the hearing of a particular word. The word he used was "Samaritan." The words associated with this term no doubt came out of her Sunday school and church experience. The words were "kind," "loving," "merciful," "Jesus," etc. No doubt to most Christians today the term "Samaritan" tends to evoke a picture of a "Christlike man of compassion" or "a good man who cares for others." As a result, it is difficult for Christians today to sense the meaning of the parable in its original setting, for the term "Samaritan" was understood in a totally different way in Jesus' day. The Jew despised the Samaritans and cursed them. A good example of this attitude is found in John 8:48, where Jesus' opponents slandered him as follows: "Are we not right in saying that you are a Samaritan and have a demon?" The Jews in general sought to avoid all contact with Samaritans. This went to the extreme that in order to avoid such contact when traveling from Judah to Galilee or vice versa, instead of simply proceeding north or south and traveling through Samaria, they would proceed eastward across the Jordan River and then proceed north (or south) until they had passed Samaria and then recross the Jordan River. In so doing, they would avoid treading upon Samaritan soil! It is not surprising, therefore, to find that the Samaritan woman said to Jesus,

> "How is it that you, a Jew, ask a drink of me, a woman of Samaria?" For Jews have no dealings with Samaritans. (John 4:9)

There are several reasons for this animosity. Some of these were: (1) After the death of Solomon in 922 B.C., the ten northern tribes led by Jeroboam revolted against God's anointed king, the son of Solomon—Rehoboam—and divided the nation. This nation of "rebels," which destroyed the unity of God's people, was known at various times as Israel, Ephraim, and Samaria. The Samaritans of Jesus' day were therefore the descendants of these rebels who destroyed the unity of God's people and the great glory of the united monarchy. (2) In 722 B.C. Samaria fell and went into exile. It was the policy of Assyria to scatter their defeated enemies throughout their territories in order to prevent organized resistance from forming. As a result of this scattering, the ten northern tribes are frequently referred to as the "ten lost tribes of Israel." The members of the ten northern tribes who remained in Samaria consisted in general of the peasantry and lower classes who gradually intermarried with the various foreigners (Gentiles) scattered in their land by the Assyrians. As a result the Jews looked down upon the Samaritans as "half-breeds." (3) After their return from exile in Babylon, the Jews, under the leadership of Haggai and Zechariah, began to rebuild their Temple in Jerusalem. The Samaritans offered to assist them in the rebuilding of the Temple, but for various reasons this offer was snubbed, and with the snub the Samaritans sought to hinder the reconstruction of the Temple (Ezra 4 to 6). (4) Having been rejected a share in the new Temple in Jerusalem, the Samaritans built their own temple on Mt. Gerizim. This temple was destroyed around 128 B.C. by the Jews under the leadership of John Hyrcanus. (John 4:20 may very well be an allusion to this.) (5) Sometime between A.D. 6 and 9 at midnight during the Passover, certain Samaritans scattered the bones of dead men throughout the court of the Temple in Jerusalem and thus defiled it.[7] The result of all this was that Jewish-Samaritan relations were filled with much tension and great animosity.

> Between the Jews and this heretical mixed people there reigned implacable hatred. On the Jewish side it went so far that they cursed the Samaritans publicly in the synagogues, and prayed to God that they should have no share in eternal life; that they would not believe the testimony of a Samaritan nor accept a service from one. This hatred was fully reciprocated by the Samaritans.[8]

The question raised by the lawyer in Luke 10.29 must also be understood as a contemporary issue that was greatly debated. Generally it was agreed that under the term "neighbor" a Jew should reckon his fellow Jews and full proselytes (the semiconvert or God-fearer was not included), but in certain circles the description of who was one's neighbor was drawn more narrowly. Pharisees tended to exclude non-Pharisees, and Essenes tended to exclude all those who were not members of their sect and even required that a man should "hate all the sons of darkness" (1QS 1:10), i.e., all those outside the sect whether they were Jews or Gentiles. Jesus quoted a popular attitude that prevailed in his day when he said, "You have heard that it was said, 'You shall love your neighbor and hate your enemy'" (Matt 5:43).

It is evident from the above that to see the parable of the good Samaritan as a beautiful, lovely example of Christian love for one's neighbor is to lose sight of the context of the first *Sitz im Leben* in which it was uttered. On the contrary,

> the parable is not a pleasant tale about the Traveler Who Did His Good Deed: it is a damning indictment of social, racial, and religious superiority.[9]

In its original *Sitz im Leben* the parable is a powerful attack against racial and religious bigotry as well as a new revelation of the limitless dimension of the command to love one's neighbor. In his command as well as in his parable Jesus removed every limitation to the love command. No one can be excluded! The neighbor we are to love is anyone—publican, sinner, Samaritan, Gentile, or enemy! Our concern is not to be in delimiting who qualifies for our love but in our being loving to all.

III. SEEK TO UNDERSTAND HOW THE EVANGELIST INTERPRETED THE PARABLE.

One of the first tasks in seeking to understand the way in which Luke used and interpreted the parable of the good Samaritan is to ascertain his redaction of the tradition. If we assume with certain form critics that Luke was the one who joined the parable of the pericope to the love command, then we shall interpret his theological emphasis in this passage somewhat differently than if we assume that his redactional work was minimal. Assuming for the sake of argument a minimum rather than a maximum of redactional work in Luke 10:25-37, it would appear that Luke, simply by selecting this parable and the love command for inclusion in his Gospel, emphasizes two themes found throughout his work.

One emphasis of Luke in his Gospel is to demonstrate the love and grace of God toward the outcasts of society. In Luke, more than in any other Gospel, we have described the loving concern of Jesus for tax collectors (3:12; 5:27-32; 7:29, 34; 15:1; 18:10-14; 19:7), sinners (5:30-32; 7:34, 36-50; 15:1-2, 7, 10; 18:13; 19:7), the poor (4:18; 6:20; 7:22; 14:13, 21; 16:19-31; 18:22; 19:8), enemies (6:27-36 is far more extensive than its parallel in MATT 5:43-48), widows (2:37; 4:25-26; 7:11-17; 18:1-8; 20:46-47, 21:1-2), the poor, maimed, lame, blind (7:22; 14:13, 21; cf. 4:18), Samaritans (10:33; 17:16; cf. Acts 1:8; 8:1, 5, 9, 14; 9:31), shepherds (2:20), thieves (23:39-43), etc. It is helpful here to note how Luke, in his redaction of the parable of the great supper (LUKE 14:15-24), has added the reference to the poor, maimed, blind, and lame being invited (v. 21), so that the parable now serves as an illustration of Jesus' teaching in Luke 14:12-14, where the believer is taught that when he prepares a banquet he should especially seek to invite the poor, the maimed, the lame, and the blind! It is important here also to note the way in which Luke portrays the coming of Jesus on the scene. Immediately after his baptism and temptation, Jesus comes to Nazareth and reads:

> The Spirit of the Lord is upon me,
> because he has anointed me to preach good news to the *poor*.
> He has sent me to proclaim release to the *captives*
> and recovering of sight to the *blind*,
> to set at liberty those who are *oppressed*,
> to proclaim the acceptable year of the Lord.
>
> (Luke 4:18-19, italics added)

The coming of Jesus upon the scene is for Luke the inauguration of the era of salvation for the outcasts. For Luke it is clear that "the Son of man came to seek and to save the *lost*" (Luke 19:10, italics added). It is also clear that the parable and the pericope of the love command fit well with the Lukan theme that the time of salvation had come and that whereas the religious elite (such as the priest and the Levite) have rejected their invitation, the outcasts of Israel (such as the Samaritan) have accepted and now share in the Messianic banquet (LUKE 14:15-24; cf. also Luke 7:29-30)! In return these outcasts love their neighbors and exhibit in miniature the love and mercy that their heavenly Father has exhibited toward them (6:36). This love does not seek to limit its recipients in any way, for it is not concerned with whom to love but with loving (Luke 10:30-37 and LUKE 6:27-36).

A second theme found in Luke involves the generous use of possessions. Love is manifested by the wise use of one's possessions to perform acts of love (6:30, 34-35; 7:36-50; 12:13-21, 33-34, 41-48; 16:1-9, 10-12, 13, 19-31; 18:18-30; 19:1-10, 11-27; 21:1-4). The Samaritan manifests these qualities of self-giving love both in his care of the wounded man as well as in his use of his possessions. Without thought of himself he uses his oil and wine to treat the wounds, binds the wounds with his headcloth or linen undergarment which he tore for this purpose,[10] pays the innkeeper sufficient money to take care of the wounded man for some time,[11] and assures the innkeeper that any additional debt which might be incurred would be paid for by him. Truly this Samaritan loved his enemies, did good, and lent, expecting nothing in return (6:35).

IV. SEEK WHAT GOD IS SAYING TO US TODAY THROUGH THE PARABLE.

It is clear that the parable of the good Samaritan teaches us to love our neighbor and that this love is to be unconditional and unqualified. The parable rejects all prejudice and discrimination whether it be racial, intellectual, financial, religious, nationalistic, etc., which in any way would restrict our doing acts of love. Since the command to love one's enemies does not refer primarily to an emotional feeling of goodwill but rather to doing acts of love, as the synonymous parallelism of LUKE 6:27-28 clearly reveals, all Christians are under the direct command of God to act lovingly toward even their enemies. The portrayal of the man who loved his neighbor as a Samaritan indicates that even the hatred of our enemies should not overcome our desire to love them. Futhermore, the Lukan understanding of God's loving concern for the outcasts of society and the needy reveals that we are especially to perform acts of love to the outcasts of our society today and to those who are in need.

The specific application of this love may vary according to our situation. In the racially tense South of the 1950s it may be that the Christian should have especially sought to do acts of love for the black who was badly discriminated against. The translation of this parable in Clarence Jordan's *The Cotton Patch Version of Luke and Acts* reveals something of how the teaching of this parable might be interpreted in such a situation.

> A man was going from Atlanta to Albany and some gangsters held him up. When they had robbed him of his wallet and brand-new suit, they beat him up and drove off in his car, leaving him unconscious on the shoulder of the highway.
>
> Now it just so happened that a white preacher was going down that same highway. When he saw the fellow, he stepped on the gas and went scooting by.
>
> Shortly afterwards a white Gospel song leader came down the road, and when he saw what had happened, he too stepped on the gas.
>
> Then a black man traveling that way came upon the fellow, and what he saw moved him to tears. He stopped and bound up his wounds as best as he could, drew some water from his water-jug to wipe away the blood and then laid him on the back seat. He drove on into Albany and took him to the hospital and said to the nurse, "You all take good care of this white man I found on the highway. Here's the only two dollars I got, but you all keep account of what he owes, and if he can't pay it, I'll settle up with you when I make a pay-day."[12]

It it obvious that such an interpretation of the parable would not have been welcomed in some of the white churches of the South in the 1950s and 1960s, and those who acted lovingly to the outcasts discovered, like Jordan and our Lord, that such behavior frequently received the response, "Crucify him!"

In Germany in the late 1930s and early 1940s, the fulfillment of this parable's teachings might have meant a special concern to act lovingly toward the Jew. Perhaps in Nazi Germany the parable should have been interpreted as follows:

> A man was going down from Berlin to Frankfurt to attend a political rally for the Führer. In Leipzig he was beaten by thieves and left dying in the streets. An official of the Nazi party saw him and as he passed by thought, "In our camps we know how to take

care of such vermin." Later the pastor of the Lutheran Church nearby saw him and as he passed by thought, "It never ceases to amaze me how depraved and fallen some men really are." But by chance there also passed a Jew who when he saw him had compassion and took him to his ghetto. There he told his friends, "I cannot stay here to care for this man because my family is being sent to Auschwitz and I must go and be with them, but here is one hundred marks. Take this money and care for him. If there is any additional expense, I promise that somehow I shall get it to you."

Needless to say such a parable would have not been considered a beautiful example of how Christians should love their enemies. On the contrary, for those who would teach in this way there would be persecution and the concentration camp.

In America in the early 1970s, the application of this parable's teaching might mean seeking to do good to the college activist demonstrating against the Vietnam war or the bewildered policeman struggling to keep order. One thing is clear. We cannot choose whom we shall have as our neighbor. Rather, we must seek actively to be a neighbor and to love all. But we must especially seek to love those who are the most oppressed and the most in need. As we reflect over the meaning of this parable, for whom should we especially prove to be a neighbor? Is it our cranky next-door neighbor? Is it the starving child in a far-off land whose name we do not know? Is it the person next door who just lost a job? Or is it . . .? Until the parable speaks to us on this level, we shall never really know what it is teaching. We may know a great deal about the parable by having applied the first three principles of interpretation, but we shall never really know what the parable "means," i.e., its significance, until we discover what God is saying to us today through this parable.

CHAPTER 7

THE KINGDOM OF GOD
AS A PRESENT REALITY

THIS CHAPTER and the succeeding ones address themes found in the parables of Jesus. A specific parable dealing with the theme of the chapter will be examined in detail. Then one or more additional parables in which the same teaching is found will be referred to.

THE PARABLE OF THE GREAT SUPPER (LUKE 14:15-24)

The particular parable chosen to typify Jesus' teaching concerning the arrival of the kingdom of God is the parable of the great supper. The parable reads as follows:

> When one of those who sat at table with him heard this, he said to him, "Blessed is he who shall eat bread in the kingdom of God!" But he said to him, "A man once gave a great banquet, and invited many; and at the time for the banquet he sent his servant to say to those who had been invited, 'Come; for all is now ready.' But they all alike began to make excuses. The first said to him, 'I have bought a field, and I must go out and see it; I pray you, have me excused.' And another said, 'I have bought five yoke of oxen, and I go to examine them; I pray you, have me excused.' And another said, 'I have married a wife, and therefore I cannot come.' So the servant came and reported this to his master. Then the householder in anger said to his servant, 'Go out quickly to the streets and lanes of the city, and bring in the poor and maimed and blind and lame.' And the servant said, 'Sir, what you commanded has been done, and still there is room.' And the master said to the servant, 'Go out to the highways and hedges, and compel people to come in, that my house may be filled. For I tell you, none of those men who were invited shall taste my banquet.'" (LUKE 14:15-24)

In MATT 22:1-10 and the Gospel of Thomas 64 we also have parables of a great banquet which possess both similarities and differences with this parable in Luke. The similarities are as follows: the scene of the parable is a feast of some sort; all the invited guests refuse to attend the banquet; a two-stage invitation is portrayed;[1] those originally invited are portrayed as giving excuses as to why they are not able to participate (not found in Matthew); the man/king is angered (not found in GT); other people are invited by the servant(s) from the streets to participate in the banquet in place of those who refused; and the parable is linked to the kingdom of God/heaven (not found in GT). There are, however, numerous differences in these three accounts as well. In Matthew it is not merely a banquet but a marriage feast which a king gives for his son. In Matthew, furthermore, there are no excuses made for not attending the marriage feast, whereas in the Gospel of Thomas four excuses are given which are all different from the three mentioned in Luke. In Matthew we also have the king's servants (in Luke and GT only one servant is mentioned) treated shamefully and killed, so that as a result the king sends his troops to kill those who treated him in this manner and to destroy their city. In Luke the servant proceeds out twice to invite replacement guests. The contexts in which the parable is placed also differ in all three works. It is clear, therefore, that despite the similarity of the setting—a banquet—there are several important divergencies in the three accounts.

In the light of the above, what conclusions can be made as to how these parables are related? It is generally recognized that the parables in Matthew and Luke do not come from a common source.[2] By this is meant that one Gospel did not serve as the source for the other Gospel (Matthew for Luke or Luke for Matthew) or that Q did not serve as the source of this parable in Matthew and Luke. This conclusion seems reasonable, for even with recognition of the redactional activity of the Evangelists the amount of editorial activity that would be required by Matthew, Luke, or both to explain the differences in these two parables would appear to be inordinate. A more likely explanation for the differences in these parables is that they are two independent variants (three, counting GT) of the same basic parable of Jesus. If this is true, it is probable that the Lukan version of the parable is more authentic. Attempts to delineate the particular sources used by Matthew and Luke (Q and M or Q and L) in their presentation of this parable have been, however, unsuccessful. Another possible explanation is that Matthew and Luke are referring to two separate parables uttered by Jesus which both used a banquet meal as a setting. The Gospel of

Thomas clearly is an independent variant of the same parable as found in Luke, so that only two parables (Matthew and Luke/GT) would need to be postulated by this explanation. It would appear presumptuous to be too dogmatic concerning either of these two alternatives, although most scholars seem to believe that all three parables are versions of the same original parable.

The Historical Setting of the Parable

In seeking to understand the teaching of this parable in Luke 14, we shall find it helpful to note some of the customs that were involved in the giving of a banquet in first-century Palestinian Judaism. Unlike the Greeks, who usually ate three meals during the course of the day, and the Romans, who usually ate four,[3] the Jews of Palestine ate only two meals.[4] The first was a late breakfast which was eaten around 10 A.M.; the second was eaten in the evening when there was no longer sufficient light to work.[5] Customarily a banquet would be held in the evening, and it should be noted that the term which is translated "banquet" in Luke 14:16, 17, and 24 is frequently translated in the New Testament as "supper." Only men would be invited to such a banquet.

According to custom, two invitations would be sent to the guests. Sometime before the actual feast the host would send his servant(s) to announce to the guests the forthcoming festivities. This is referred to in v. 16, where we read, "A man once gave a great banquet, and invited many." The above statement corresponds to the first invitation that would be sent out, [6] for "the repetition of the invitation at the time of the banquet is a special courtesy, practised by upper circles in Jerusalem."[7] The second invitation would be brought by the servant(s) on the actual day of the feast to inform the guests that all was now ready. This second invitation is referred to in v. 17, where we read:

> And *at the time for the banquet* he sent his servant to say to those who had been invited, "Come; for all is now ready." (LUKE 14:17, italics added; cf. also Esth 5:8; 6:14)

Once the banquet started, there was a period of time in which late guests were still permitted to enter and participate in the banquet, but after the introductory courses were completed, the welcome sign that was hung from the house was removed. After this, late guests were no longer welcome (cf. Matt 25:1-13).[8]

It is evident from the above that the parable of the great supper is drawn from the life and customs of first-century Palestinian Judaism.

To say this does not mean that some of the actions portrayed in the parable are not unusual. To have all the invited guests refuse to come (v. 18) is most unusual, but in a parable unusual actions such as this are frequently portrayed and would be accepted as part of the storyteller's freedom in telling the story. As for inviting others to the banquet, this is quite possible since common sense would suggest that the food should not be wasted and the Jewish emphasis on the giving of alms to the poor (compare Jesus' teaching in Luke 14:12-14) would indicate that such behavior as described in the parable could easily be envisioned. Jeremias even recounts a rabbinic story of a rich tax collector, Bar Ma'jan, who was received into heaven because he once made a banquet for the city councillors and when they refused to attend, he invited the poor to eat, that the food not be wasted.[9] For this God rewarded him!

The Point of the Parable in the First Sitz im Leben

In seeking to ascertain the particular point which Jesus was making in this parable, we must look at the various "figures" involved in the story. There are essentially four such figures: the man who gave the supper; the guests who refused to attend; the replacements who attended; and the supper itself. Around which of these figures does the parable revolve? How should we name this parable to emphasize the main point? Should it be called "the parable of the irate master"? In so naming the parable we would make the master the key figure and emphasize that the main point would be in the anger of the master (no doubt God) over the rejection by his guests (no doubt the leadership of the Jewish nation) of the kingdom of God. Or should we name it "the parable of the disobedient guests"? Here we would place the emphasis upon the guests' (the leadership of Israel) rejection of the kingdom of God. If we name it "the parable of the replacement guests," we would be emphasizing the giving of the kingdom of God to the outcasts of Israel (and the Gentile world). It should be noted that this theme is found in the parable of the evil tenants (MARK 12:1-11). On the other hand, the parable could be named, as it usually is, "the parable of the great banquet." Here the emphasis is placed upon the banquet itself, and the response of the guests and the replacement of these guests would be understood in the light of the arrival of the great banquet.

That "the parable of the great banquet" is the best title for this parable and that the banquet receives the primary emphasis is evident for at least two reasons. Within Judaism, and later in Christianity, the metaphor of a banquet or supper was frequently used to portray the bliss of the age to come. The future messianic age, however it was conceived, was symbolized as involving a "messianic banquet." We find this metaphorical use of a supper in the Apocrypha (2 Esdras 2:38), the Pseudepigrapha (Enoch 60:7f.; 62:14), the Dead Sea Scrolls (1QSa 2:11-23), as well as in the rabbinic literature (Midrash Genesis 62:2; b. Sanhedrin 153a). Within the Gospels also we find that the bliss of the future age was symbolized in Judaism as a supper (MATT 8:11; Luke 14:15). In Christianity this image was picked up and adopted to portray the present realization of the kingdom of God (1 Cor 11:23-26; MARK 14:22-25) as well as the future consummation when the believer will sit at the table with the risen Christ and share in his kingdom (MARK 14:25; LUKE 22:30; Rev 19:9). It would appear, therefore, that Jesus' use of the metaphor of a banquet would quite naturally have been interpreted eschatologically as a reference to the messianic banquet.

A second argument in favor of this interpretation is Luke 14:15. Although the arrangement of LUKE 14:15-24 after Luke 14:7-14 is no doubt Lukan, there is little reason to assume that the statement concerning the bliss of eating bread in the kingdom of God is from the hand of Luke.[10] Whatever the origin of v. 15a ("When one of those who sat at the table with him heard this, he said to him . . ."), the statement in v. 15b ("Blessed is he who shall eat bread in the kingdom of God!") is traditional rather than editorial and could quite possibly describe the actual occasion of the parable.[11] In its present context in Luke the great banquet referred to in the parable must be related to the bliss of those who will share in the messianic banquet and "eat bread in the kingdom of God." The point of the parable therefore must also deal with the eating of bread in the kingdom of God, i.e., the coming of the kingdom of God and the messianic banquet. In this regard it should be noted that in MATT 22:1-10 the parable begins as follows:

> The kingdom of heaven may be compared to a king who gave a marriage feast for his son. (MATT 22:2)

It is clear that the parallel parable in Matthew also has as its main point the comparison of the kingdom of heaven to a marriage feast.[12] If this parable is in fact a variant of the same original parable as LUKE 14:15-24, then we have additional support for our conclusion that the central point of comparison in the parable is the comparison of the kingdom of God (or heaven) to a great supper.

Within the parable there are three specific "refusals." Linnemann has argued that the refusals should not be taken as absolute rejections but rather as excuses for coming late.[13] She lists several arguments in favor of this view. The most important are that the invited guests are not offering weak excuses which are meant to be deliberate slights to the host and that vs. 21-24 demonstrate that the invitation to fill the hall with the men of the streets and lanes has as its purpose filling the house, so that when the original guests do come there will be no room for them. Jeremias has rightly objected to this interpretation for a number of reasons.[14] For one, v. 20 cannot be interpreted in any way as a desire to come late but must be understood as a deliberate refusal. This Linnemann acknowledges, but she seeks (as she must) to interpret this verse as a later addition to the parable. There are no real compelling grounds for doing this, however. Secondly, Jeremias points out that the parallel accounts of this parable in Matthew and the Gospel of Thomas (as well as the alleged rabbinic parallel that he gives of Bar Ma' jan, the rich tax collector) all understand the reactions of the guests as refusals. Finally, in addition to these arguments of Jeremias, it should be pointed out that, unlike the parable of the wise and foolish maidens (Matt 25:1-13), we do not read of any attempt by the guests to arrive late and participate in the banquet. It seems, therefore, more logical to see the replies of the invited guests as refusals to come to the banquet.

What was Jesus' purpose, then, in telling this parable? As we have already noted and will observe again, Jesus often used his parables as an apologetic for his activities. Should this parable perhaps then be interpreted, like the parables of the lost sheep (LUKE 15:4-7), the lost coin (Luke 15:8-10), the gracious father (Luke 15:11-32), and the laborers in the vineyard (Matt 20:1-16), as a vindication by Jesus to his critics of his preaching the good news to the poor and the outcasts of Israel? Or should we interpret this parable primarily as a proclamation that indeed the messianic banquet (or the kingdom of God) had come? The setting given in Luke 15:1-2 to the parables of the lost sheep, the lost coin, and the gracious father is clearly one in which Jesus' activity in proclaiming the good news to the outcasts of Israel is being challenged. The present context of our present parable, however, favors an eschatological interpretation, for the setting given for the parable in v. 15 is a statement about the joy of participating in the bliss of the kingdom of God. The setting of Luke 14:15 is therefore not one in which Jesus must defend himself, but rather one in which he comments concerning the bliss of eating bread in the eschatological kingdom and the parable which follows should therefore be interpreted as teaching about that kingdom. The parable furthermore ends, not with a defense over the lost sharing in the joy of the banquet but with a reference to the final judgment (cf. Luke 11:8; 15:7, 10; 16:9; 18:8, 14) and the final consummation of the messianic banquet (cf. here Luke 22:30 and the final sentence of the parallel in GT 64). It would appear best, therefore, to intepret the parable primarily as an eschatological proclamation rather than as an apologetical defense.[15]

An attempt has been made to interpret this parable along the lines of a midrash based on Zeph 1:1-16 in which the coming of the Messiah is likened to a holy war.[16] According to this interpretation, the excuses offered by the guests are all legitimate according to Deuteronomic regulations for exclusion from normal warfare (see especially Deut 20:5-7), but the invitation is not for a normal war but rather for the final religious holy war, so that these excuses are not valid here. As a result, even the custom of sending food from the banquet table to those who cannot attend will not be practiced.[17] Although this interpretation does recognize the eschatological nature of the parable, it is not convincing. The main problem with this interpretation is that LUKE 14:15-24 does not refer anywhere to a military expedition of any sort. Any such reference must come from the Matthean parallel to this parable. Yet we have pointed out that the differences between Matthean and Lukan accounts are due either to their having come from two separate parables of Jesus or to their coming from two separate accounts of the same parable, and if the latter is true, the Lukan account is surely more authentic.[18]

According to the Lukan context, sometime in the ministry of Jesus at a banquet (14:7-14), a pious platitude was uttered which spoke of the bliss of eating in the kingdom of God. No doubt the statement was made by one who was reasonably confident, because of his keeping of the law, of his own invitation to and participation in that great event when the devout of Israel would sit at table with Abraham, Isaac, and Jacob in the kingdom of God (MATT 8:11). For him the kingdom of God was clearly a future, otherworldly reality yet to come. However, Jesus' message was clear. In his ministry the kingdom of God has come![19] Whereas this man would never have consciously rejected an offer to share in the messianic banquet but, on the contrary, would have professed that his great desire and goal was to participate in the kingdom of God, he was blind to the realization that he was in fact doing just that! Jesus' message of "Repent, for the kingdom of heaven is at hand" (Matt 4:17) was nothing less than the pronouncement "Come; for all is now ready" (LUKE 14:17). Linnemann rightly states,

"Any opposition that does not do justice to this 'Now is the acceptable time' (cf. 2 Cor 6:2) has missed the sense of the parable."[20]

Jesus in the parable warns that the kingdom of God has come, and if one is not willing now to heed the summons, it will mean exclusion. What good is it to know how to interpret the signs of the sky, if one is not able to discern the signs of the time (MATT 16:2-3)? How ironic it is that the children of the kingdom are rejecting the offer and that the "dogs" are not participating (MARK 7:27-28) and being compelled to come in.[21] Strange as it may seem, it is those who one would least expect to participate in the kingdom of God that are now entering into the messianic banquet.

The kingdom has come! If those invited exclude themselves from the kingdom, then others will take (and are taking) their place. The excuses offered appear quite valid, excuses for rejecting Christ and his kingdom frequently do, but the result is the same—exclusion from the kingdom! The arrival of the kingdom clearly brings with it an absolute demand. All earthly priorities vanish away in its presence, for the kingdom carries with it an absolute demand. It is no coincidence that Luke 14:25-33 follows this parable. The demand of the kingdom is absolute. The point of the parable for Jesus, however, lies not so much with the demand of the kingdom, for most people would have accepted the view that God's demand is absolute. What Jesus is interacting with here is the concept that the kingdom of God is future—"Blessed is he who *shall* eat bread in the kingdom of God." The kingdom has already come, however. The table is already prepared and all is now ready. The invitation has gone forth. It is inappropriate to talk about participation in the kingdom in the future tense. Now is the time of salvation! If the religious elite of Israel will not enter the kingdom now, it will be too late. They will never taste the banquet, and others will take their place!

It is impossible in reading this parable not to interpret the guests and their replacements as representing the attitudes of the Pharisees/scribes/religious leaders and the outcasts of Israel. Does this, then, make this parable an allegory? It would appear that in the first *Sitz im Leben* the parable was not allegorical, because it posits only one main point of comparison. The point is that the kingdom of God has come and that those who would have been expected to receive it (the religious elite) did not do so, whereas the ones least likely to receive it (the publicans, poor, harlots, etc.) have. At this stage the parable is not yet an allegory, for every parable contains a basic comparison of one thing (a banquet which is rejected by some and received by others) with something else (the coming of the kingdom of God which is rejected by the religious elite and received by the outcasts). The parable therefore contains only one basic comparison, but we shall see that Luke did add an allegorical element to it.

The Interpretation of the Parable by the Evangelist

It has already been suggested that the location of the parable of the great banquet after Luke 14:7-14 is probably the work of Luke. This may be true. If so, no doubt the primary reason for this placement was thematic, since both accounts deal with the theme of a banquet of some sort. Yet far more important than the arrangement of the two accounts for ascertaining the Lukan redactional emphasis is the description of the new guests invited to the banquet. Unlike the parallels in Matthew and the Gospel of Thomas, Luke has two invitations to the new guests. In the first invitation Luke explicitly states that those invited are to be the poor, the maimed, the blind, and the lame. Here Luke mentions the same four classes of guests that the believer is told to invite to his banquet in Luke 14:13 (cf. also Luke 4:18; 7:22). This passage, which has no parallel in Matthew, and the fact that the parallel in the Gospel of Thomas does not describe the replacement guests in this manner indicate that the explicit fourfold description of these guests is Lukan. We have, furthermore, already pointed out that one of the theological concerns of the third Evangelist was for the poor and the outcasts of the world.[22] In contrast to the Matthean and Gospel of Thomas parables in which nothing is said about the people who are invited as replacements to the banquet, Luke emphasizes once again the gracious offer of the gospel to the disadvantaged. In so doing he has added to the eschatological proclamation of the parable a hortatory dimension as well.

Additional editorial activity can be seen on the part of Luke in the sending out of the servant a second time to find additional guests for the banquet (v. 23). This second invitation, which is lacking in the accounts in Matthew and the Gospel of Thomas, indicates that whereas the emphasis in the Matthean parable falls heaviest on the exclusion of those who rejected the invitation to the banquet, in Luke the emphasis falls more upon the inclusion of the outcasts in the banquet. This, as we have seen on several occasions, is a Lukan theological emphasis. It is furthermore difficult not to see in this twofold invitation an allegorical element, for after the servant has gone out and collected guests from "the streets and lanes of the city" he is commanded to go out farther to "the highways and hedges" and to compel others to come to the banquet. No doubt for Luke the parable is to be understood as teaching that due to the rejection of the gospel by the Jewish leadership, the gospel has been given to the outcasts of Israel (the streets and lanes of the city) as well as to the Gentiles (the highways and hedges).

If the above is correct, we need not interpret this to mean that Luke has confused or corrupted the original intention of the parable. It is far better to see in Luke's redaction an inspired application of this parable to the situation which Luke faced in his day. The explicit concern for the poor and the outcasts was already hinted at by Jesus in the parable. After all, what kind of people could this servant find at the last minute in the streets and lanes (v. 21) and invite to the banquet? Would it not be the poor, the maimed, the blind, and the lame? What Luke has simply done is to make explicit what was implicit in the parable and the teachings of Jesus elsewhere. As for the second invitation, Luke again took that which was implicit and at times only alluded to in the teachings of Jesus[23] but in the light of the Gentile mission of his day made this explicit. Yet surely the Gentiles fit well the image of the outcasts (v. 21) now invited to share the banquet. If Luke is guilty of anything, it is in his explicating what the parable of Jesus meant for the audience to which he was writing, and in this he had "the mind of Christ" (1 Cor 2:16).

ADDITIONAL PARABLES OF PRONOUNCEMENT

Wedding Feast and Fasting (MARK 2:18-20)

We have another parable in which the metaphor of a feast is used to describe the coming of the kingdom of God:

> Now John's disciples and the Pharisees were fasting; and people came and said to him, "Why do John's disciples and the disciples of the Pharisees fast, but your disciples do not fast?" And Jesus said to them, "Can the wedding guests fast while the bridegroom is with them? As long as they have the bridegroom with them, they cannot fast. The days will come, when the bridegroom is taken away from them, and then they will fast in that day." (MARK 2:18-20)

The setting given for this parable involves the practice by the Pharisees and the followers of John the Baptist of fasting which stood in stark contrast with the disciples of Jesus who did not practice this esteemed rite in Judaism. The Pharisees fasted twice a week (Luke 18:12), and Mondays and Thursdays were set aside especially for this purpose.[24] Why was it that Jesus' disciples did not practice this aspect of Jewish piety? The question clearly assumes that this behavior by the disciples was not accidental but intentional and was based upon some theological ground.

In his reply to this question Jesus makes use of traditional Jewish images and customs. The use of the metaphor of a marriage feast brought with it many connotations. Even as the covenant at Sinai was likened to a marriage of the nation to YHWH and the Torah to a marriage contract, so too, the final renewal of the covenant in which the kingdom of God was to be realized was perceived in Judaism as the time when the true marriage would take place.[25] In the parable Jesus also alludes to the custom by which attendants at a wedding were excused from certain religious obligations, such as fasting, during the wedding festivities in order not to interrupt the rejoicing.

That the parable is in effect a pronouncement that the behavior of the disciples is due to the arrival of the kingdom of God is clear for a number of reasons. First of all, the image of the wedding feast which Jesus uses was a common metaphor in Judaism for the coming of the kingdom of God. The use of this metaphor by Jesus does not in and of itself, of course, demand an eschatological interpretation, but in the context of his pronouncement that the kingdom was now a present reality such an interpretation seems best. Secondly, Jesus used this same metaphor elsewhere to designate either the realization of the kingdom of God in his ministry or the consummation of the kingdom when the Son of man would return.[26] Finally, it should be noted that the explicit contrast between the established pattern of Jewish practice (fasting) and the practice of Jesus' disciples (feasting) must be explained in some way. The explanation of Jesus does not condemn the past practice of fasting as being wrong. He simply states that it is past, i.e., it is obsolete. Fasting does not fit the present time. Why? The only answer is that the bridegroom is now present and the wedding has begun. In the light of Jesus' other teaching concerning the coming of the kingdom of God in his ministry, what else can this mean than that the kingdom of God has arrived?[27]

Finally, it should be noted that in the parables/metaphors which follow there is an explicit contrast between the new patch/wine and the old garment/wineskin. Our parable agrees well with this theme in that the practice of fasting (the old) is contrasted with the practice of feasting (the new). The placement of these parables together reveals at the very least that Mark and/or the early church interpreted them similarly, so that the eschatological nature of MARK 2:21-22 argues for a similar eschatological interpretation of this parable.

Why then do the disciples of Jesus not fast? The reason is that they cannot! How can they fast during the time of celebration and rejoicing? The kingdom of God has dawned. In the coming of Jesus the messianic time of rejoicing has begun, and the disciples, "poor in spirit" (MATT 5:3) and "persecuted for righteousness' sake" (Matt 5:10), know that "theirs is the kingdom of heaven." The great wedding feast so long awaited has begun; the time of salvation that the truly devout of Israel have longed for has come (Luke 2:25-37). The parable must be understood therefore as a proclamation that the kingdom of God has come and that the practice of the disciples of Jesus is due to this conviction.

Patch (MARK 2:21); New Wine and Old Wineskins (MARK 2:22)

Following this parable we find two additional parables:

> No one sews a piece of unshrunk cloth on an old garment; if he does, the patch tears away from it, the new from the old, and a worse tear is made. (MARK 2:21)

> And no one puts new wine into old wineskins; if he does, the wine will burst the skins, and the wine is lost, so are the skins; but new wine is for fresh skins. (MARK 2:22)

Although it is uncertain as to when these two sayings were joined together and connected with the preceding parable, it is clear that for Mark they belong together with the parable of the wedding feast. In reading the two parables together, it appears at first as if the contrast portrayed in the two sayings is different from the contrast in the previous parable, for here the contrast is temporal (new vs. old) whereas in the parable of the wedding feast the contrast is qualitative (feasting vs. fasting). Upon closer examination, however, it is clear that the contrast is essentially the same, for in all three parables it is essentially the incompatibility of two opposing realities that is portrayed. Feasting does not go with fasting; a new patch does not go with an old garment; and new wine does not go with old wineskins. The contrasts are therefore much closer than it may appear at first glance. Having noted this similarity, we must still ask why Jesus used these three examples of incompatibility. What has happened that makes the practices of Judaism "old"? The answer of Jesus is clear—"The kingdom of God has come upon you" (LUKE 11:20). To use Pauline terminology we can say, "The old has passed away, behold, the new has come" (2 Cor 5:17).

Mustard Seed (MARK 4:30-32); Leaven (MATT 13:33)

These two additional parables deal with this same theme:

> And he said, "With what can we compare the kingdom of God, or what parable shall we use for it? It is like a grain of mustard seed, which, when sown upon the ground, is the smallest of all the seeds on earth; yet when it is sown it grows up and becomes the greatest of all shrubs, and puts forth large branches, so that the birds of the air can make nests in its shade." (MARK 4:30-32)

> He told them another parable. "The kingdom of heaven is like leaven which a woman took and hid in three measures of flour, till it was all leavened." (MATT 13:33)

In seeking to understand these parables, we must be on our guard not to permit Western ideas of progress and growth to be read into the parable. No doubt such ideas, ultimately stemming from a Hegelian philosophy that dominated theological as well as all kinds of thinking in the last century, have caused these parables to be interpreted as teaching an evolutionary growth of the kingdom of God. According to this view the kingdom of God (often seen as embodied in such teachings as the Fatherhood of God, the brotherhood of man, the reign of God in the human heart) has begun with Jesus, and now it is growing and will continue to grow until all the world will manifest the inner rule of God in the human heart. Such evolutionary optimism was dealt a mortal blow by the cannons of World War I, the pen of Karl Barth, and subsequent events such as World War II, the Korean War, the Vietnam war, and places like Auschwitz, Buchenwald, the Gulag Archipelago, Cambodia, etc., have nailed the coffin shut upon such naive optimism. They have also helped us to rethink these two parables, and as a result it has become clear that they teach something quite different from an evolutionary growth of the kingdom of God. In the Oriental mind, and we must remember that Jesus belongs more to the Orient than to the West, the parables are seen as contrasting the beginning and the end rather than as portraying a progress. Surely this emphasis and way of reading the parables is correct, since no progress report is given.[28] The comparison that is made is between a small mustard seed, proverbial in the East as the smallest of seeds,[29] and the final product — a large bush—and between flour unleavened and flour after it is leavened. It is clearly in the contrast between the end and the beginning that the point of these parables is to be found.[30]

The point of these parables then must be found in the contrast between the insignificant beginning of the kingdom of God and its final glory.[31] Yet we can be even more specific than this. The main emphasis does not lie in the greatness of the kingdom of God in its final manifestation, for every Jew who heard Jesus would agree to this. To claim that the kingdom of God in its consummation at the end of time would be great and glorious would be little more than a tautology for a Jew. Of course it would be. It could be nothing else since it was the kingdom of *God*. What was not recognized nor understood was the smallness and insignificance of its beginning. How differently and unexpectedly has the kingdom of God come. Rome is oblivious to its arrival, and even the Jewish leaders are blinded by their own religiosity. They cannot conceive that the wedding has begun and that such disreputable characters as the harlots, the publicans, the poor, the blind, are already now participating in the blessings of the kingdom. Although they have eyes, they do not see; although they have ears, they do not hear (MARK 4:12). For them the kingdom of God is hidden.[32]

Weather Signs (LUKE 12:54-56); Divided House (MARK 3:22-27)

Here are two additional parables that proclaim a similar message and should be observed together:

> He also said to the multitudes, "When you see a cloud rising in the west, you say at once, 'A shower is coming'; and so it happens. And when you see the south wind blowing, you say, 'There will be scorching heat'; and it happens. You hypocrites! You know how to interpret the appearance of earth and sky; but why do you not know how to interpret the present time?" (LUKE 12:54-56)

> And the scribes who came down from Jerusalem said, "He is possessed by Beelzebul, and by the prince of demons he casts out the demons." And he called them to him, and said to them in parables, "How can Satan cast out Satan? If a kingdom is divided against itself, that kingdom cannot stand. And if a house is divided against itself, that house will not be able to stand. And if Satan has risen up against himself and is divided, he cannot stand, but is coming to an end. But no one can enter a strong man's house and plunder his goods, unless he first binds the strong man; then indeed he may plunder his house." (MARK 3:22-27)

In the first parable Jesus condemns the crowds because of their ability to discern the signs of the weather but their lack of discernment concerning the signs that were associated with Jesus' ministry.[33] Seeing the cloud(s) coming from the west, they were able to ascertain that they were filled with moisture from the Mediterranean Sea, so that when these moisture-laden clouds passed over the Shephelah and the mountains of Judah the cooler temperatures of the hill country would cause the moisture to condense and rain would water the earth. On the other hand, they also knew that a southern wind blowing from the desert would bring with it the heat of the parched desert. If that wind were from the southeast, they could even tell that a dreaded sirocco was coming, bringing with it exceedingly high, dry winds and oppressive heat.

Yet other "signs" were taking place and they were oblivious to their significance. The possessed were being delivered of their demons. The rule and dominion of Satan was crumbling, for one greater than Satan was present. What was the significance of Satan's house and goods being plundered (MARK 3:27)? Why were the crowds unable to "interpret the present time" (LUKE 12:56)? Satan was being defeated in their very presence. What else could this mean than that the promised kingdom of God, in which Satan's defeat was promised,[34] had now come? How could they not realize that

> if it is by the finger of God that I [Jesus] cast out demons, then the kingdom of God has come upon you. (LUKE 11:20)[35]

If ignorance were the main cause of this lack of perception, this might be excusable, but the lack of perception was due not to ignorance but to hypocrisy (LUKE 12:56). Not to see the signs of the times would indeed be worthy of rebuke, but the opponents of Jesus did see the signs! They did acknowledge that indeed the demons were being vanquished and the possessed were being delivered. But instead of acknowledging the coming of the kingdom of God, they assessed this divine blessing as evil and the work of Satan (MARK 3:22). The foolishness of such logic was clear (MARK 3:23-27). For Satan to destroy his very own work was absurd. For him who had eyes to see, it was evident that the antithesis of Satan was present, overcoming and destroying his kingdom. What else could this mean but that the reign of God had begun? It was because of their hardness of heart and their refusal to acknowledge the inbreaking of the kingdom of God that they were "hypocrites" and their sin damnable. It was because of this rejection of the work of the Spirit of God in their hearts and of his work in the ministry of Jesus that they were "guilty of an eternal sin" (MARK 3:29)!

CONCLUSION

In the light of the parables discussed above it seems clear that Jesus thought of his ministry as inaugurating the kingdom of God. With the coming of John the Baptist, the kingdom had come near; in his own coming on the scene, the long-awaited kingdom had arrived! Already the messianic banquet had begun and while the religious elite of Israel were excluding themselves, the poor and maimed, the blind and lame, the publicans and sinners were now participating (LUKE 14:15-24). The present time could not therefore be one of fasting, for fasting would be anachronistic in this time of feasting and joy (MARK 2:18-20). Yet "anachronistic" is not a strong enough term. This coming of the kingdom was new and unique. One must not seek to confuse the previous period of the Law and the Prophets with the present time (LUKE 16:16). To do so would be like sewing an unshrunken piece of cloth to an old garment or like pouring new wine into old skins (MARK 2:21-22). The religion of Judaism was now "old," i.e., an old covenant; the new covenant had begun and with it came the new wine.

It may well be that the coming of the kingdom of God seems insignificant and small, but its small beginning should not be minimized! The kingdom is nevertheless here. Like the small grain of mustard seed or the small morsel of leaven, it is a present reality, and while it is small now its consummation will be great indeed (MARK 4:30-32; MATT 13:33). Yet, although the kingdom has not come as many had anticipated and although it has not yet shaken the earth, for those who have eyes of faith, the signs are evident. The present ruler of this world has been cast out (John 12:31), for his kingdom has been overthrown and his captives released (MARK 3:22-27). For those with eyes to see, the long-awaited kingdom of God has come.

CHAPTER 8

THE KINGDOM OF GOD AS DEMAND— THE CALL TO DECISION

THE KINGDOM OF GOD has come! Already now the longed-for kingdom has entered history in fulfillment of the Old Testament promises. Although its presence seems small and insignificant, it is nonetheless a present reality and foreshadows the final consummation of the kingdom when history will come to an end. Already now the kingdom of God is "in process of realization."[1] Because of this "now is the acceptable time; behold, now is the day of salvation" (2 Cor 6:2). The coming of the kingdom of God brings with it the call to decision.

The Parables of the Hidden Treasure (Matt 13:44) and the Pearl (Matt 13:45-46)

This call is revealed in the twin parables of the hidden treasure and the pearl of great price:

> The kingdom of heaven is like treasure hidden in a field, which a man found and covered up; then in his joy he goes and sells all that he has and buys that field. (Matt 13:44)

> Again, the kingdom of heaven is like a merchant in search of fine pearls, who, on finding one pearl of great value, went and sold all that he had and bought it. (Matt 13:45-46)

These two parables are not found in any other canonical Gospel, but they are found in the Gospel of Thomas. There we find them in the following forms:

> Jesus said: The kingdom is like a man who had a treasure [hidden] in his field, without knowing it. And [after] he died, he left it to his [son. The] son knew nothing (about it). He accepted that field

(and) sold [it]. And he who bought it came, (and) while he was ploughing [he found] the treasure. He began to lend money at interest to [whomever] he wished. (GT 109)

Jesus said: The kingdom of the Father is like a merchant who had merchandise (and) who found a pearl. This merchant was prudent. He got rid of (i.e. sold) the merchandise and bought the one pearl for himself. You also must seek for the treasure which does not perish, which abides where no moth comes near to eat and (where) no worm destroys. (GT 76)[2]

It is generally agreed that the Gospel of Thomas is dependent on sources other than the Synoptic Gospels for these parables, so that it witnesses to another form of the tradition than we find in Matthew.[3] It is also acknowledged that the form of these two parables in the Gospel of Thomas is for the most part secondary.[4] The parables have clearly been used to expound gnostic theology. The Gospel of Thomas is useful, however, in pointing out that the sources used by it, while they contained both parables, did not place them side by side, since the parable of the hidden treasure is saying 109 and the parable of the pearl is saying 76. Several other reasons have also been given to support the view that the parables were not originally uttered together. For one, the tenses of the verbs in the two parables differ in that the first parable contains historic presents (goes, sells, buys) whereas the second uses aorists/pasts (went, sold, bought).[5] It has also been suggested that the repetition of the expression "the kingdom of heaven is like" in v. 45 and in v. 47, which begins the parable of the great net, argues against these two parables having originally belonged together.[6] As a result, it would appear that the placement of these two parables side by side is due to the Evangelist rather than to Jesus or the Evangelist's sources.

The Historical Setting of the Parable

The historical situation portrayed by Jesus in these two parables is readily understandable at first glance, although it is not without difficulty as we shall see. In the first parable a treasure hidden for some time is discovered. In ancient times the safest "bank" was a safe hiding place, for by burying his treasure the owner would protect it from being stolen by thieves or forcibly taken from him by conquering enemies. If the owner died, was murdered, or taken into captivity, such treasure would remain hidden ofttimes for centuries, until by chance it was discovered. Two questions, however, arise with respect to the behavior of the man who found the hidden treasure. One involves the legality of his behavior and the other the morality of it. These are not necessarily the same, for what may be legal in a society may not necessarily be moral or Christian. Derrett has dealt at length with the former issue,[7] and points out that according to Talmudic law "moveables," such as the hidden treasure, could only be acquired by "lifting."[8] Because of the legal situation involved in his working for the owner of the field, the finder in the parable therefore did not "lift" the earthenware jar (cf. 2 Cor 4:7) in which the treasure was no doubt hidden. Derrett and others as well point out that the man could not have been the servant of the owner of the field, since a servant's finding of the treasure would mean that the treasure automatically would belong to his master, i.e., the owner of the field. As a result the man in the parable must have been a day laborer or *sokher*. Upon finding the hidden treasure the *sokher* immediately covered it up. He was careful not to lift the treasure, for then it would become the property of the owner who was paying him for such work. He therefore covered up the treasure, purchased the field by selling all that he had, and then as owner of the field possessed the treasure for himself by lifting it.

This reconstruction has been accepted by many[9] and does provide helpful background material for understanding the parable. Yet it is far from certain that Jesus' audience would have assumed that a *sokher* was repairing a wall for the owner and proceeded exactly along the lines described by Derrett. What is clear is that they believed that the man of the parable could have acquired such treasure by the purchasing of the land in which he found the treasure. Apart from this possibility the parable would not make sense. As a result for Jesus' audience (or at least for Matthew's), whatever might be the legal aspects for acquiring such treasure, the acquisition of that treasure in the manner described in the parable was a clear possibility. Who knows? Perhaps recently something just like this had occurred and Jesus based his parable on the incident!

The question of the moral behavior of the man in the parable must also be discussed. It has been suggested by some that there was nothing immoral in the behavior of the finder.[10] This may be correct. Legally the behavior of the individual was probably "formally legitimate," but the behavior of the man, as portrayed by Derrett, in obtaining possession of the treasure falls far short of the Golden Rule. The wisest approach to this issue, however, is not to attempt to "legalize" his behavior but to realize that parables generally teach a single main point and not to press the details.[11] As has been pointed out above, in several parables of Jesus the behavior of the commended people falls short, often far short, of the ethical teachings of Jesus. In those cases as well as here one should not press these details but simply seek the main point of the parable.

In the parable of the great pearl we have a merchant seeking to buy pearls. The Greek term used to describe this "merchant" is *emporos* and indicates that the man in this parable is not a shopkeeper but a wholesale trader or dealer who was involved in the purchasing of pearls. Jeremias argues that the reference to the merchant being a dealer in pearls is secondary and Matthean because in the Gospel of Thomas parallel the man is simply described as a merchant.[12] This may be true, and warns us against emphasizing the supposedly different ways in which the treasures were found: by chance (hidden treasure) and by deliberate searching (great pearl). If the reference to the merchant being a pearl merchant is secondary, then in the *Sitz im Leben* of Jesus both treasures were found by chance.[13] Yet even if the merchant was referred to by Jesus as a pearl merchant, the difference in the method of discovery is irrelevant, for both men are surprised. Even for the merchant seeking to buy pearls it is good fortune to have found this pearl, for in seeking pearls he, to his great surprise, found not just a good pearl but *the* pearl of great price.[14]

The Point of the Parable in the First Sitz im Leben

Although there are several differences in these parables, the parable of the hidden treasure and the pearl or pearl merchant have traditionally been treated as twin parables that teach the same main point. The main differences are as follows:

1. The first parable speaks of a treasure; the second speaks of a pearl merchant rather than a pearl.

2. The first parable portrays a remarkable coincidence which is totally a surprise; the second portrays the finding of a pearl in the process of pearl buying.

3. The verbal forms in the first parable are present tenses; those in the second are aorist.

4. Different words are used to describe the "purchasing" of the field/treasure and the pearl.[15]

It is of course true that these differences exist, but they are differences primarily of style rather than of essence. The introductions ("The kingdom of heaven is like treasure . . ." and "Again the kingdom of heaven is like a merchant . . .") are not to be pressed literally, however, for such introductions are quite general in nature. Essentially these introductions should be translated as follows: "It is the case with the kingdom of God as with the following story of a treasure . . . or of a merchant who. . . ."[16] While it is therefore true that the introductions are formally different and probably reveal that they were uttered on separate occasions, this in no way changes the fact that both parables still teach the same main point. We have also pointed out above that the difference in the method of finding the treasure and pearl should not be pressed since for both the discovery was a surprise. Despite, therefore, these formal differences in the parables, they have almost universally been interpreted as twin parables which teach the same point. Certainly the least that we can say is that Matthew, who placed these parables together, understood them as twin parables, for the "again" of v. 45 clearly indicates that Matthew saw these two parables as intimately related in meaning.

There have been several suggestions as to what the main point of the parables was in the first *Sitz im Leben*. Some of the more likely possibilities see the main emphasis as lying in:

1. The *value* of the kingdom of God. (This is clearly the point of the version of the parable of the pearl found in GT 76.)

2. The *sacrifice* required to enter the kingdom of God.

3. The *joy* of sharing in the kingdom of God.

4. The *hiddenness* of the kingdom of God.

5. The need to *search* for the kingdom of God.[17]

Some of these possibilities can be eliminated rather quickly. The emphasis on *searching* is at best found only in the parable of the pearl, for the man who found the hidden treasure was not in any way searching for the treasure he found. He found it by sheer chance. The parable of the hidden treasure can therefore in no way be interpreted as emphasizing the need of search for the kingdom of God even if we are told elsewhere to "seek first his kingdom and his righteousness" (MATT 6:33; cf. 7:7). With regard to the *hiddenness* of the kingdom of God it need only be pointed out that whereas the expression "[having been] hidden" is used in the first parable, it is not found in the second. In fact there is nothing "hidden" about the pearl at all. It is in the process of purchasing that the merchant found this very valuable pearl. Others may have seen it before him, and if he did not purchase it, others would have seen it and have had opportunity to purchase it after him. It should also be noted that for Matthew the kingdom of heaven is not "hidden." On the contrary, any hiddenness about the kingdom is due not to any quality innate in the kingdom, itself, but rather to the unwillingness of people to repent and receive the kingdom. The emphasis on the *joy* of finding the kingdom of God is likewise found in only the first parable. In all these three suggested emphases we therefore find that the supposed emphasis is found explicitly in only one of the two twin parables. It would appear, however, that the common point of emphasis in these two twin parables should appear in both parables, for it seems reasonable to believe that the main point of these parables would be expressed in each of them!

In both parables we find at least two common elements that make up the "picture" part of the parable. One is that in both a precious object—either the treasure or the pearl—is found, and in both the men sold all they had to obtain this precious object. It seems clear that it is in one of these two common elements that the main point of the parables is to be found. Yet is Jesus emphasizing the *value* of the kingdom or the *sacrifice* involved in entering it? There are several reasons for concluding that it is the latter rather than the former that is being emphasized in the parable. For one, the value of the kingdom of God would be a given for both Jesus and his audience. To say that the kingdom of God is a precious reality is almost a tautology. Surely all in Jesus' audience would say, "Blessed is he who shall eat bread in the kingdom of God!" (Luke 14:15; cf. MARK 10:28-30). To emphasize the surpassing worth of the kingdom of God therefore seems unnecessary.[18] Secondly, the end stress of both parables lies with each man selling all and purchasing the treasure. It is the behavior of both men that receives the primary emphasis in the two parables. They both reacted similarly. They sold all they had to possess the treasure/pearl. This point agrees well with Jesus' teachings found elsewhere concerning counting the cost (Luke 14:28-33) involved in following him (cf. MATT 8:19-22; 10:37-38; etc.). The shift from the past tense (actually the aorist) which we find at the beginning of the parable of the hidden treasure (v. 44a-b) to the present tense at the end (v. 44c) should also be noted since this draws attention to the end of the parable, where the cost is emphasized.[19]

Linnemann has objected that the term "sacrifice" is a poor choice to describe the main point, for the decision is not a sacrifice.[20] To purchase the once-in-a-lifetime treasure/pearl is not a sacrifice at all, for to surrender something of lesser value in order to obtain the supreme value is not sacrifice. Linnemann's caveat is well taken. If we understand the term "sacrifice" as portraying a solemn, difficult, reluctant, heroic decision, then indeed we misread the parables. Whereas we have indicated that the main point of the parables is not the joy of sharing in the kingdom of God, it is nevertheless "from joy" that the man sells all that he has. It is evident, therefore, that Jesus in these parables meant to portray the decision to possess the kingdom of God as a "joyous sacrifice"! Its possession brings joy; not to sell all to possess it brings grief and sorrow as the rich young ruler discovered. "At that saying his countenance fell, and he went away sorrowful; for he had great possessions." (Mark 10:22.) The point of the parable in the first *Sitz im Leben* has been described well by C. H. Dodd.

> But with the fundamental principle in mind, that Jesus saw in His own ministry the coming of the Kingdom of God, we may state the argument thus: You agree that the Kingdom of God is the highest good: it is within your power to possess it here and now, if, like the treasure-finder and the pearl-merchant, you will throw caution to the winds: "Follow me!"[21]

In the ministry of Jesus the kingdom of God has indeed come, and in the light of this, one should sacrifice all one has to possess this great treasure.

The Interpretation of the Parable by the Evangelist

In the Gospel of Matthew it is evident that whereas the parables in 13:1-35 are addressed to the crowds, the parables of the weeds and the householder, in 13:36-52, are directed to the disciples.

> Then he left the crowds and went into the house. And his disciples came to him, saying, "Explain to us the parable of the weeds of the field." (Matt 13:36)

> And he said to them, "Therefore every scribe who has been trained for the kingdom of heaven is like a householder who brings out of his treasure what is new and what is old." (MATT 13:52)

Jeremias apparently understands these two parables as being directed to the disciples in the first *Sitz im Leben*, because he includes them under the section entitled "Realized Discipleship" rather than in the previous section entitled "The Challenge of the Hour." Yet in the situation of Jesus the parables were more a call to decision than to a continued faithfulness. The main reason for this conclusion is the once-for-all nature of the decision portrayed in the parables. The great value of the kingdom demands the supreme decision. Elsewhere this can be described as a call to "repent," "follow" Jesus, "believe," "take up the cross," "confess" Jesus, "keep his words," "take up his yoke," "lose one's life," "hate one's family," etc.[22] Here the call is figuratively portrayed as selling all. The punctiliar nature of this demand for decision surely fits well a general audience such as the crowds who heard Jesus, better than the disciples. In the first *Sitz im Leben*, therefore, it would appear that Jesus' purpose was a specific call to the crowds to enter into the kingdom of God which Jesus now offered.

Yet Matthew was not writing to the crowds and sought to apply these twin parables to his Jewish-Christian audience. In his hands the parables now served a paraenetic rather than an evangelistic function.[23] In applying these parables to his Christian audience, however, does Matthew switch the emphasis from that of sacrifice to the great value of the kingdom of heaven? Does Matthew in his use of the tradition have a similar emphasis as the writer of The Letter to the Hebrews? There are some significant similarities between these two canonical books, for both see the "new covenant" (Heb 12:24) as the fulfillment of the Old Testament covenant (Matt 5:17) and both see this covenant as a better one (Heb 7:22) which brings a better righteousness (Matt 5:20). For the writer of Hebrews, the main emphasis in his argument involves the "value" of the new covenant. He urges his readers to remain true to their commitment because of the surpassing quality of the revelation (Heb 1:1 to 4:13), high priest (4:14 to 7:28), and sacrifice (8:1 to 10:18) found in their "new" faith.

Does Matthew in his use of these two parables proceed in a similar manner? That Matthew is convinced of the great value of the kingdom of heaven goes without saying. After all, it is likened to a treasure and a pearl of great price! Yet the main emphasis that our parables receive in the third *Sitz im Leben* is similar to that which they received in the first. For Matthew it is the "sacrifice" aspect of the parables that continues to receive the main emphasis. He admonishes his readers through these parables that having found the kingdom of heaven and having committed themselves to it, they must continue in faithfulness to that commitment. He urges them essentially to "hold fast the confession of [their] hope without wavering" (Heb 10:23), "to work out [their] own salvation with fear and trembling" (Phil 2:13), to "be faithful unto death" (Rev 2:10). Having "found" the kingdom of heaven, Matthew urges his readers to stand by their "find."

For Matthew, then, the culmination of the parables of the Hidden Treasure and of the Pearl would lie in the sphere of sacrifice, or total investment, which we prefer to designate as "total commitment" (cf. 5:29f.; 8:22; 10:34-9; 18:8f.; 19:12, 21, 29).[24]

Additional Parables of Decision

The Unjust Steward (Luke 16:1-8)

Another parable that likewise emphasizes the need for a radical decision in the light of the coming of the kingdom of God is the parable of the unjust steward:

> He also said to the disciples, "There was a rich man who had a steward, and charges were brought to him that this man was wasting his goods. And he called him and said to him, 'What is this that I hear about you? Turn in the account of your stewardship, for you can no longer be steward.' And the steward said to himself, 'What shall I do, since my master is taking the stewardship away from me? I am not strong enough to dig, and I am ashamed to beg. I have decided what to do, so that people may receive me into their houses when I am put out of the stewardship.' So, summoning his master's debtors one by one, he said to the first, 'How much do you owe my master?' He said, 'A hundred measures of oil.' And he said to him, 'Take your bill, and sit down quickly and write fifty.' Then he said to another, 'And how much do you owe?' He said, 'A hundred measures of wheat.' He said to him, 'Take your bill, and write eighty.' The master commended the dishonest steward for his shrewdness; for the sons of this world are more shrewd in dealing with their own generation than the sons of light." (Luke 16:1-8)

The authenticity of this parable is seldom debated, for its very difficulty guarantees its authenticity. In seeking to understand the point of this notoriously difficult parable, the interpreter encounters a number of serious problems. Stated simply they are:

1. Where does the parable actually end?
2. Why was the steward called "dishonest"?
3. Is the behavior of the master conceivable?
4. To what kind of audience did Jesus address this parable?

Only when these questions are answered can we hope to ascertain the point of the parable.

1. *Where does the parable actually end?* Integrally related to this question is the question of to whom "the master" of v. 8a refers. Does this

refer to the "master" of vs. 3 and 5 or to Jesus himself? If it refers to Jesus, then the parable proper ends at v. 7, but if it refers to the master of vs. 3 and 5, then the parable ends at v. 8a, 8b, or 9. Luke 18:6 is often suggested as a parallel to v. 8a, and in 18:6 it is clear that at the end of the parable of the unjust judge the expression "the Lord" refers to Jesus.[25] One can also compare here Luke 12:36-37 and LUKE 12:41-46 where the expressions "Lord" and "the Lord" refer to Jesus in vs.41f. but in vs. 36-37 refer to God, and Luke 13:23 and 25f. where again "Lord" refers to Jesus in the one instance (the former) and to the householder in the other. In all these instances, however, there is no confusion as to where the parables end and what "Lord" refers to in each instance. Furthermore, in Luke 18:1-8 the term "Lord" does not appear in the parable itself, and it is clear from the context that the parable has ended at 18:5, so that the analogy is far from exact. There are at least three reasons for interpreting "the master" of Luke 16:8 as a reference to the "master" of vs. 3 and 5. The first is that there is present in our account no attempt to distinguish them! Unless there is good reason to distinguish the use of "master" in v. 8a from vs. 3 and 5, we should assume that they refer to the same person. This is the normal procedure in seeking to understand the meaning of terms in a passage. Without a clear discrimination between the third use of "master" and the first two uses, we must assume that they refer to the same individual. Secondly, in 16:9 the shift from the third person to the first person ("And I tell you . . .") indicates a change in subject from "the master" of v. 8. Attempts to minimize this argument by pointing to instances where a shift from indirect speech to direct speech does occur[26] are not convincing. Generally such changes as we find in vs. 8 and 9 do reveal a change in the speaker (cf., for example, Luke 18:9-13 and 18:14), and there is no reason to reject this general rule in this instance. Finally, it should be pointed out that if "the master" of v. 8a refers to Jesus, the parable then ends at v. 7 with great abruptness and without any real conclusion.[27] The parable requires v. 8a as its conclusion! In the light of the above it seems clear that "the master" of v. 8a refers to "the master" of vs. 3 and 5 and that the parable originally contained v. 8a.[28] It would also appear, as most scholars maintain, that vs. 8b-13 are a Lukan arrangement of authentic sayings of Jesus which he used to provide an interpretation of the parable for his audience, but we shall for the moment defer further discussion of this until later.

2. *Why was the steward called "dishonest"?* The second question that we must deal with involves the actions of the steward. In v. 8a he is referred to as "the dishonest steward." Is he dishonest because of what

he has just done in vs. 5-7, i.e., cutting the bills, or because of previous actions? In Luke 18:6 the "unrighteous judge" is referred to in this manner because of his previous actions, and in our parable we read in vs. 1-2 that the steward is told to turn in the accounts of the stewardship because of the charges of wasting his master's goods that have been brought against him. Yet whereas it is clear that the steward is being discharged and that this "firing" was justified (the "quickly" of v. 6 indicates that he has little time left to act and that the master has good grounds for discharging him), it is unclear as to whether the charges for this firing involved ineptness or dishonesty. Either could be the grounds for his dismissal, or for that matter both might have served as the grounds. It is far from certain, however, that the description of the steward in vs. 1-2 demands that he be described as "dishonest." A great deal of discussion has been raised as to exactly what the steward did in vs. 5-7. The traditional interpretation has been that the steward falsified the debts owed his master in favor of the debtors so that when he was discharged by his master he would then be able to "collect" on the favors owed him by the debtors. In so doing he was indeed cheating his master for the sake of ensuring his future. Others have suggested that

a. The steward was simply eliminating the interest which his master was collecting on the principal. This action by the steward was strictly legal since the charging of interest, while practiced broadly, was legally forbidden by the Torah. Thus he gained favor with his debtors.[29]

b. The steward was simply eliminating his personal profit or commission from the bill.[30] In this way, the master lost nothing and he gained the goodwill of the debtors. Decisive against this view are the financial considerations involved. According to Jeremias, the amounts that each of the two bills was reduced was approximately five hundred denarii.[31] It also appears from v. 5 "one by one" and v. 7 "to another" (not "the other") that more than two debtors were involved! How would the steward's forgoing his commissions for the sake of the goodwill of the creditors help prepare him better for the future than pocketing those commissions, which for the two debtors alone amounted to one thousand denarii? It should be noted in this regard that according to Matt 20:2 a denarius was a day's wage. The two debtors alone therefore owed the steward over three years' salary! If indeed the moneys eliminated from the bills were the steward's commission, both the actions of the steward in forgoing these commissions and his panic in v. 3 are unexplainable. This explanation is unacceptable unless it can be shown that all the steward's commissions would be forfeited by his losing his position. Kenneth Ewing Bailey has pointed out another decisive criticism of this interpretation in that any such commissions by the steward would not appear on the master's bill but be "below the table,"[32] and the steward has the debtors change *the master's bills,* so that what the debtors owed was owed the master, not the master and the steward. Note here the questions of vs. 5 and 7, "How much do you owe *my master?*" (italics added).

c. The steward cut the bills of the debtors in order that they would respond favorably toward both him and his master, and his master now in turn would not countermand this change for fear of losing the goodwill of the debtors.[33] A general consideration that weighs against this interpretation is its complicated nature. Could Jesus' audience be expected to supply all the additional bits of information needed to complete this interpretation? This seems unlikely. It seems reasonable to assume that the present form of the parable contains all that is necessary for the reader to arrive at its main point. It does not appear likely that Luke or Jesus would have presumed so much additional information on the part of their audience. Most decisive against this view, however, is that it conflicts with the stated reason of his actions in v. 4!

An important consideration against any attempt to legalize the actions of the steward is the reference to his being "dishonest" in v. 8. The steward is not called dishonest in vs.1 and 2. He could simply be inept or careless. "At any rate, the point of 'injustice' is not made clearly enough so that v. 8 can be a reference back to a known quality of the steward."[34] It has also been pointed out that the characterizing genitive in v. 8a ("dishonest") is not needed in v. 8 since it is clear which steward is being referred to. However, if something in vs. 3-7 has helped reveal a particular quality of "dishonesty" about the steward which is central to the parable, then such a description is necessary. Consequently, it seems reasonable to conclude that the term "dishonest" in v. 8 could and probably would have been omitted if it did not refer to the actions of the steward in vs. 3-7, since apart from these verses this designation is totally unnecessary. Its inclusion therefore describes not so much the reason for the charges being leveled against the steward, but his subsequent behavior. It would appear as a result that the traditional interpretation of why the steward was called "dishonest" has the most to commend it.

3. *Is the behavior of the master conceivable?* A third problem involved in the interpretation of this parable is the response of the master to the

steward's action. The difficulty is obvious, for how can one commend someone for cheating him? It almost looks as though the master is commending dishonesty. That the master's response is unexpected and unusual is obvious. Yet is it impossible to imagine? It is not inconceivable to imagine an Oriental potentate who with a wry smile could say: "You shrewd rascal! You have always prepared yourself for every emergency, and here you have done it again. You certainly are a clever and resourceful scoundrel. Be off and never darken my door again!"[35] That such a response would be considered unusual goes without saying, but the parables of Jesus are filled with examples of unusual behavior. It is frequently this very unusual and unexpected behavior that typifies Jesus' genius as a storyteller. While the behavior of the master is unusual, the hearers of the parable could accept it in a parable.

4. *To what kind of audience did Jesus address this parable?* At first glance the issue seems clear and simple. Luke 16:1 says that it was addressed to the disciples! Yet the point of the parable as well as Luke 15:1-2 and 16:14 seems to imply that the Pharisees are also his audience. In 15:1-2 the Pharisees and scribes are mentioned as the audience to which the parables of the lost sheep, the lost coin, and the gracious father are addressed, and in 16:14 it appears that the Pharisees heard "all this," i.e., Luke 16:1-13. On the other hand we must acknowledge that the arrangement of all this material is Lukan and that he may be seeking to take certain materials that were addressed to a hostile audience such as the Pharisees and scribes and apply them to the followers of Jesus. It appears that the parable of the dishonest steward may be an example of this. Jeremias states:

> If, as v. 8a suggests, it is a summons to resolute action in a crisis, it would hardly have been addressed to the disciples, but rather to the "unconverted," the hesitant, the waverers, the crowd. They must be told of the imminent crisis: they must be urged to deal with it courageously, wisely, and resolutely, to stake all on the future.[36]

What, then, is the point of the parable in the *Sitz im Leben* of Jesus? The key to Jesus' thinking must lie in v. 8a. This is true regardless of whether v. 8a refers to Jesus' own interpretation of the parable, i.e., if "the master" refers to Jesus, or whether it is part of the parable itself. Surely the stress of this parable comes at the end. The dishonest steward is commended. But for what? Clearly it is not for his dishonesty. Rather, it is for his "prudence" or cleverness.[37] This prudence does not necessarily demand honesty or godliness but is rather "non-moral cleverness and skill deployed in self-preservation."[38] This is evident by the way the term is used in such passages as: MATT 7:24; 10:16; Matt 25:2; Rom 11:25; 12:16. The man in our parable had the cunning cleverness to prepare for the judgment awaiting him from his master. He acted wisely by preparing for his future in the light of the crisis he faced. He was prudent or shrewd because by his actions people would receive him into their houses when he was put out of his stewardship (v. 4). Jesus by this parable urges his audience to be prudent also. He had announced that the kingdom of God had come and with it came blessing for the "poor in spirit" and judgment for the self-righteous. "Even now the axe is laid to the root of the trees; every tree therefore that does not bear good fruit is cut down and thrown into the fire." (LUKE 3:9.) In the light of this judgment, which is imminent and already dawning, the hearers should be prudent like the dishonest steward and prepare themselves now. "Act now, so that you will be received into the eternal habitations." Jeremias sums up the point of the parable well when he says:

> You are in the same position as this steward who saw the imminent disaster threatening him with ruin, but the crisis which threatens you, in which, indeed, you are already involved, is incomparably more terrible. This man was . . . [wise] (v. 8a), i.e., he recognized the critical nature of the situation. He did not let things take their course, he acted unscrupulously no doubt. . . . Jesus did not excuse his action, though we are not concerned with that here, but boldly, resolutely, and prudently, with the purpose of making a new life for himself. For you, too, the challenge of the hour demands prudence, everything is at stake.[39]

Luke in his redaction takes this point of Jesus and applies it to his audience. For the followers of Jesus there is also a need to act prudently. Since the parable involves bills, debts, money, Luke appends to the parable various sayings of Jesus dealing with money in vs. 9-13 and one that urges the followers of Jesus to act prudently with regard to their own material well-being. That this is a favorite Lukan theme is evident from the following parable of Lazarus and the rich man (Luke 16:19-31), LUKE 12:32-34, and the general treatment of riches in Luke-Acts.[40] Again, however, rather than seeing in the Lukan redaction a misinterpretation of Jesus' main point, we should see here the application of this point—being prudent in preparing oneself for the kingdom of God—to the church's situation in his day with respect to riches.

The Tower, and War (Luke 14:28-32)

We have two additional twin parables that deal with our theme.

> For which of you, desiring to build a tower, does not first sit down and count the cost, whether he has enough to complete it? Otherwise, when he has laid a foundation, and is not able to finish, all who see it begin to mock him, saying, "This man began to build, and was not able to finish." Or what king, going to encounter another king in war, will not sit down first and take counsel whether he is able with ten thousand to meet him who comes against him with twenty thousand? And if not, while the other is yet a great way off, he sends an embassy and asks terms of peace. (Luke 14:28-32)

In Luke these two parables are placed in the context of the conditions for discipleship addressed to the crowds (14:26, 27, 33). That this arrangement is Lukan can be seen from the fact that whereas vs. 26-27 are Q material, i.e., found together also in MATT 10:37-38, the parables themselves are L material, i.e., found only in Luke. This conclusion has been made even more certain by the discovery of the Gospel of Thomas, for here we find the equivalent of Luke 14:26-27 in saying 55 and this is disassociated from our two parables.[41]

Although the arrangement of Luke 14:25-33 is due to the Evangelist, his interpretation and use of these twin parables is essentially the same as that of Jesus. Whereas at times Jesus appeared to discourage potential disciples from following him (cf. MATT 8:18-20), what he was discouraging was not following him but following him without "counting the cost." The kingdom of God is offered graciously by God to all. Exclusion from it is due not to the difficulty of "earning" entrance but rather to the willful rejection of the gracious invitation (cf. here LUKE 14:15-24). Yet the grace of God is not "cheap grace." It is grace pure and simple, but it is a commitment to the rule of grace in one's life. One can only receive the grace of God with open hands, and to open those hands one must let go of all that would frustrate the reception of that grace. Jesus refers to this letting go as repentance. In our parables he told his audience that they should consider what this repentance involved before they received the grace of the kingdom, for it was foolish and damning to seek entrance into the kingdom without first considering carefully if one is willing to repent. "No one who puts his hand to the plow and looks back is fit for the kingdom of God." (Luke 9:62.) (Cf. here also what the writer of Hebrews states in Heb 6:4-6!) One must "count the cost," i.e., consider carefully, whether he is willing to renounce all in order to receive the gracious offer of the kingdom which God is extending to him.

Several other parables that deal with the same demand for decision can only be listed here. These are the parable of reconciliation with an accuser (LUKE 12:58-59); the parable of the guest without a wedding garment (Matt 22:11-14); the parable of the wise and foolish builders (MATT 7:24-27); and the parable of the soils (MARK 4:3-9). The latter has frequently been interpreted as an encouragement and assurance to the disciples that the kingdom of God had indeed come and, "in spite of every failure and opposition, from hopeless beginnings, God brings forth the triumphant end which he had promised."[42] There are several reasons, however, for questioning this interpretation which rejects the canonical interpretation of the parable found in MARK 4:14-20. For one, it would appear that the amount of space devoted in this parable to the other three soils (vs. 3-7) cannot be ignored. In contrast to a single verse devoted to the good soil, we have five verses devoted to the other soils. This seems to be an inordinate amount of space to devote simply to the stage setting or "local coloring" of the parable's main point. Furthermore it should be noted that the average length of each of the first three soils is actually greater than the length of the description of the good soil! Secondly, the question of the eschatological nature of the harvest has received much discussion of late. If the harvest is associated with the individual seeds rather than the entire field, the harvest is by no means that extraordinary since a single seed can produce a thirty-sixty-hundred-fold harvest.[43] Another argument in favor of the traditional interpretation of this parable is that it fits the context of a mixed audience (MARK 4:1-2, 9, 10) and the canonical interpretation well. Finally it must be questioned whether too much emphasis has been placed on the end stress of this parable. The present writer cannot help questioning if a different order would really change the point of the parable that much. If the parables were told with the good soil coming first, much of the art of telling the story would be lost, but would its point be any different? Probably not! In the light of all this, it would appear that the parable of the soils is best understood as teaching the need for a proper reception of Jesus' message of the kingdom of God, i.e., a faithful hearing of Jesus' words (MATT 7:24-27), and should be entitled the parable of the soils rather than the parable of the sower.

CONCLUSION

Within this chapter we have sought to demonstrate that integrally related to Jesus' proclamation that the kingdom of God had in fact come was a concomitant teaching that this coming demanded decision. Even as Joshua and the prophets after him could call Israel to "choose this day whom you will serve" (Josh 24:15), so Jesus called his hearers to decision. At times this decision can appear at first glance simply as the eternal need to decide for or against God (cf. LUKE 12:58-59; MATT 7:24-27). Yet to interpret the parables of decision in this way is to disconnect them from their eschatological ground. Something new has occurred. The kingdom of God has come. Therefore now as never before the call goes out to choose. The treasure of the kingdom, the pearl without price, can now be yours. Be not fools and exclude youselves. *Be prudent!* With joy rid yourselves of everything that hinders you from receiving the gracious offer of God. Now is the time! Why hesitate any longer?

CHAPTER 9

THE GOD OF THE PARABLES

THE KINGDOM OF GOD has come and with it comes the call for decision. But what kind of God is it that calls people to decision? Is he a God who in his holiness and glory brings judgment and wrath, whose glory and righteousness brings damnation to the unrighteous? That God is holy and just and must judge the world was, of course, a postulate accepted by all of Jesus' audience and in our next chapter we shall see that the message of the parables is in part one of judgment. Yet the day of vengeance of our God is still future. This is now the acceptable year of the Lord.[1] Now is the time of repentance, and the very fact that Jesus calls his audience to repent reveals the graciousness and mercy of God since he is obligated neither to give such an opportunity nor to accept man's repentance. In the parables, as well as in the rest of Jesus' teachings, the gracious character of God is constantly revealed.

THE PARABLE OF THE GRACIOUS FATHER (LUKE 15:11-32)

One of the parables in which we find this portrayal of God is the parable of the gracious father:

> And he said, "There was a man who had two sons; and the younger of them said to his father, 'Father, give me the share of property that falls to me.' And he divided his living between them. Not many days later, the younger son gathered all he had and took his journey into a far country, and there he squandered his property in loose living. And when he had spent everything, a great famine arose in that country, and he began to be in want. So he went and joined himself to one of the citizens of that country,

who sent him into his fields to feed swine. And he would gladly
have fed on the pods that the swine ate; and no one gave him
anything. But when he came to himself he said, 'How many of my
father's hired servants have bread enough and to spare, but I
perish here with hunger! I will arise and go to my father, and I will
say to him, "Father, I have sinned against heaven and before you; I
am no longer worthy to be called your son; treat me as one of your
hired servants." ' And he arose and came to his father. But while
he was yet at a distance, his father saw him and had compassion,
and ran and embraced him and kissed him. And the son said to
him, 'Father, I have sinned against heaven and before you; I am no
longer worthy to be called your son.' But the father said to his
servants, 'Bring quickly the best robe, and put it on him; and put a
ring on his hand, and shoes on his feet; and bring the fatted calf
and kill it, and let us eat and make merry; for this my son was dead,
and is alive again; he was lost, and is found.' And they began to
make merry.

"Now his elder son was in the field; and as he came and drew
near to the house, he heard music and dancing. And he called one
of the servants and asked what this meant. And he said to him,
'Your brother has come, and your father has killed the fatted calf,
because he has received him safe and sound.' But he was angry
and refused to go in. His father came out and entreated him, but he
answered his father, 'Lo, these many years I have served you, and
I never disobeyed your command; yet you never gave me a kid,
that I might make merry with my friends. But when this son of
yours came, who has devoured your living with harlots, you killed
for him the fatted calf!' And he said to him, 'Son, you are always
with me, and all that is mine is yours. It was fitting to make merry
and be glad, for this your brother was dead, and is alive; he was
lost, and is found.' " (Luke 15:11-32)

One question that must be raised at the very beginning in the
investigation of this passage is whether we are dealing here with one
parable or with two. It is evident that the parable has a natural break or
division at 15:25. Do we have then in our passage two separate
parables, one about a prodigal son and the other about an older
brother, which Luke has brought together for the first time? Or has
Luke perhaps created the second part of the parable (vs. 25-32) as an
interpretative addition to the original parable which he found in the
tradition?[2] Or is the entire passage a two-part parable which is
traditional and goes back to Jesus himself? It would appear upon closer
examination that Luke 15:11-32 is not a composite of two independent
parables for at least two reasons. One reason is the fact that whereas

15:11-24 could stand by itself (hence the familiar title "the parable of the prodigal son"), the latter verses cannot, but demand something like 15:11-24 to render them intelligible. Secondly, even in vs. 11-24 we find mention of two sons, and if vs. 25-32 were not part of the original parable, only one son would need to be mentioned.[3]

More recently the question has been raised as to whether the second part of our present parable is an entirely Lukan creation. The main argument in favor of this thesis is linguistic. According to Jack T. Sanders the first part of our parable contains numerous non-Lukan grammatical and vocabulary traits whereas the latter verses (15:25-32) contain a "heavy concentration of specifically Lukan terms and meanings."[4] This criticism has been attacked by a number of scholars,[5] and it seems reasonable to conclude that "the case against Lukan composition of 15:11-32 would seem to be fairly conclusive."[6] It should also be noted that, although in the parable the older brother represents the Pharisees and scribes, the treatment of the older brother in the parable is amazingly gentle and mild. He is even portrayed as possessing a privileged position over his repentant younger brother. Surely if the creation of this latter portion of the parable were due to the hand of Luke, the portrayal of the older brother would have been different, for in this day the gospel had now been clearly rejected by Israel and had passed to the Gentile world. If Luke had created this part of the parable, he no doubt would have treated the older brother in the same way that so many interpretations of the parable treat him—as lost and also in need of repentance and forgiveness. The moderate treatment of the older brother in the parable fits far better the *Sitz im Leben* of Jesus than of Luke.[7] It would appear therefore that whereas in the parables of the lost sheep and the lost coin Jesus in justifying his eating with publicans and sinners did so by demonstrating God's joyous reception of the lost, in our parable he also sought to demonstrate the lovelessness and hardheartedness of his opponents.

A second issue that must be dealt with before we investigate the historical setting of the parable involves whether the parable is an allegory or not. That one can and must see in the attitude of the main characters of the parable various qualities of the Pharisees/scribes, publicans/sinners, and God is obvious. One cannot help seeing in the older brother of the parable the embodiment of the Pharisees and scribes who murmur, "This man receives sinners and eats with them" (15:2). And surely the father in his great love and mercy portrays the love and mercy of the God Jesus proclaimed. The prodigal also recalls to mind the publicans and sinners who had sinned grievously against

God and who were frequently in the service of Gentiles (cf. v. 15). Yet despite these analogies it is clear that we have in Luke 15:11-32 a story parable and not an allegory, for although the father is clearly representing the character of God,[8] he is also clearly distinguished from God. This is most evident in vs. 18 and 21 when the prodigal says, "Father, I have sinned against heaven [i.e, God] and before you." It is likewise evident that the parable is not an allegory, despite its long history of allegorization, because the details have no essential symbolic meaning attached to them. The parable therefore remains a parable with a basic point of comparison. The fact that the father, the younger son, and the older son represent or characterize the God of Jesus, who is reaching out in mercy to the publicans and sinners to the irritation and consternation of the Pharisees and scribes, does not make this parable into an allegory, for we are still dealing with a single basic comparison.[9]

The Historical Setting of the Parable

As we have observed above, our parable speaks of a father and two sons. The younger son, who was probably around seventeen years of age since it appears that he was unmarried,[10] asks for "the share of property that falls to me" (15:12). The use of the definite article indicates that he is referring to a specific inheritance that he might expect to receive one day. According to the law (Deut 21:17) the younger son would receive upon the death of his father one third of the inheritance in contrast to two thirds for the firstborn or older brother. Before the death of the father, however, it is extremely unlikely that the younger brother would receive the full one third of the inheritance. It has been suggested that the younger son would not have received any of the land itself but only a share of the disposable possessions of his father,[11] but the terminology of the parable that describes the bestowal of the inheritance ("he [the father] divided his living between them" and "the younger son gathered all he had") indicates that the property as well as the disposable assets were divided between the two sons. Because of future needs, which would be involved in maintaining the dependents of the family, especially any unmarried daughters, the father would probably not have given the full one third which the younger son might have expected at his father's death. As a result it has been suggested that two ninths of the inheritance might be a more likely amount. At this time the older son was also given his share of the property, as 15:12c clearly states, but no doubt the father would have protected himself by maintaining the right of use until his death. In the Talmud we read of the estate being given to the son(s) "from today—but after my death."[12] We might say that the property was now vested to the older brother, but that the father still preserved the usufruct. Thus the father can later say to his older son "all that is mine is yours" (15:31) in that, although he enjoyed the use of his property during his lifetime, it legally belonged to his firstborn. No doubt the father would have done this at least in part to protect the inheritance rights of the older son from any possible future claim of the younger brother who had received his inheritance already and had nothing more coming.

Although the parable does not state specifically why the younger son asked for[13] his inheritance, several suggestions have been made. Some have suggested that there was nothing impertinent or evil in the younger son's desire, but that we should see here an analogy in our own century of younger sons who left Europe or Asia to come to America in order to make their fortune. Opportunities were limited in Judea and with over four million Jews living in the diaspora in comparison to the one-half million living in Judea, the younger son simply sought to make his fortune under the siren call "Go west, young man; go west!"[14] Bailey, however, has pointed out that in every Middle Eastern culture where he has told this parable, the universal conclusion of his hearers was that the younger son hated his father and wanted him to die.[15] He also points out that in no Middle Eastern literature, past or present, is there an example of a younger son asking for his inheritance from a father who was in good health. As a result the argument given above that the son was simply seeking to make his fortune and in no way was insulting his father appears to be invalid. The text itself also gives the impression that the son's motive for seeking his inheritance was less than noble, in that we do not read in v. 13 that he lost his money by means of poor investments or even by theft. On the contrary we read that "he squandered his property in loose living." The text therefore suggests the traditional view that the "prodigal son" wasted his living on "wine, women, and song" (cf. v. 30). Attempts to ennoble the younger son's actions in order thereby to protect the father's character (For is not such a father foolish to give to his rebellious son his inheritance to squander away?) are unnecessary. That the father's action was generous to the point of being foolish and does not provide a wise pattern to follow in all instances is obvious, but we must remember that we are dealing with a parable and should not press the details!

The younger son soon dissipates his fortune in his revelry only to realize too late that he had played the fool. Now a famine comes upon the land, and the prodigal, in the depths of sin, adds apostasy to his other sins by "joining himself to one of the citizens of that country" (note the analogy here of publicans who have joined themselves in service to the Gentiles, i.e., Rome) and feeding swine. In regard to the latter the Talmud states, "Cursed be the man who would breed swine."[16] It is hard to imagine a more effective portrayal of depravity for first-century Judaism which could serve as an example for Jesus of the greatness of God's love of the sinner. Yet the portrayal continues. "And he would gladly have fed on the pods that the swine ate" (15:16). In his hunger the prodigal is pictured as wanting to eat with the cursed swine and share their "table," and yet he remained hungry.[17] At this stage the prodigal "came to himself." Jeremias has pointed out that what follows in the parable is a vivid description of what it means to repent.[18] The prodigal first of all acknowledged his guilt, and the twofold nature of that guilt as well as the order of his acknowledgment must be observed: "I have sinned against heaven and before you." The prodigal "had sinned against Heaven . . . and in the sight of his father, for appropriately, he had disobeyed the fifth commandment and at one and the same time injured both God and his father."[19] By his dissipation the prodigal had sinned, for he had not loved God with all his heart and his neighbor (in this case his father) as himself (Mark 12:29-31). The prodigal then turned away from his present situation and in hope (for he remembers the gracious and loving character of his father) he returns: "I will arise and go to my father" (15:18).

In the father's actions toward his son we should note the artistic portrayal of this scene by Jesus. Even before the prodigal is able to give this prepared speech "his father saw him and had compassion, and ran and embraced him and kissed him" (15:20). For an Oriental father to run to his son in this way is not only extremely unusual but considered undignified.[20] Yet such is the love of God that Jesus seeks to portray in the parable. Other actions of the father, which although not allegorical display in Jesus' culture the full acceptance of the prodigal by the father, follow. These are the kiss of reconciliation (cf. 2 Sam 14:33); the placing of the best robe upon him; the giving of a ring (probably a signet ring); and the placing of sandals upon his feet. All of this indicates the father's full acceptance of the prodigal as his son and the bestowal of authority upon him.[21] There then follows a feast, the joy of which is described in the synonymous parallelism repeated twice in the parable—"for this my son was dead, and is alive again; he was lost, and is found" (15:24, 32). By these overt actions the father reveals to his household and the community as well, which were both probably quite hostile toward the prodigal for the way he had dishonored his father, that his son's past is forgotten. The prodigal is his son, and his father's honor and protection are upon him.

The parable does not end, however, at this point. There is an older brother! Again the artistry of Jesus must be noted. The elder son's absence during the reconciliation and the beginning of the feast is well staged. His refusal to join the feast as he learns of the occasion beautifully portrays the attitude of Jesus' opponents (cf. LUKE 14:15 24) as does the disrespect of the older son toward his father in 15:27, 29. Throughout the parable titles of address have been used up to this point. The absence of a title of address by the older son to his father is therefore most noticeable. The older son, despite all his claim of loyalty to his father's commands (15:29), does not give his father the loving respect that he deserves. He is more concerned with his father's commandments than with his father! Surely Jesus in this portrayal had in mind those religious enthusiasts of his day (and this is equally true today) who kept the jot and tittle of what they thought was the law of God but whose hearts were nevertheless far from him. Finally we must note how the older brother refers to his younger brother—"this son of yours" (15:30). To argue that the prodigal was the son of another wife is surely beside the point in the light of 15:32. The older brother simply will not acknowledge the prodigal as his brother. Again Jesus has brilliantly captured and portrayed the attitude of his opponents, the Pharisees and scribes, who would in no way accept their fellow Jews who were publicans and sinners as brothers.[22]

Yet what was the elder brother's problem in accepting his younger brother? It has been suggested that the older brother was worried that the acceptance of the younger brother would take away from his future inheritance.[23] This, however, cannot be the real issue, for the estate is legally vested to the older brother alone (15:30) and nothing is made of this issue in the parable. Most telling against this interpretation is the fact that the "picture part" of the parable, the older son's animosity, would not then correspond to the "reality part" of the parable, the animosity of the Pharisees and scribes toward the publicans and sinners with whom Jesus ate, for this had nothing to do with finances. In part at least, it would appear that the very acceptance of the prodigal was a problem for the older brother. This seems to be revealed by the rejection of brotherhood in 15:30a —"this son of yours." But even more galling than the acceptance of the prodigal back, for the Pharisees and scribes did accept the fact that sinners could repent, was the way he was received back! Where there should be in his opinion sobriety, penance, remorse, sorrow, shame, sackcloth and ashes, etc., there is feasting and rejoicing. This is what is so irritating! If publicans and sinners are to enter the kingdom of God, let them do so with a penance, sorrow, and remorse appropriate to the severity of their sin! To be sure, the older brother would reason that it was his sense of rightness that demanded this, for his "brother" had insulted and shamed his father grievously. The older brother indeed had a high view of righteousness and justice but too little an understanding of mercy. Ultimately he begrudged the fact that his father was gracious and merciful (cf. Matt 20:15).

The Point of the Parable in the First Sitz im Leben

In seeking the main point of the parable, we see the one possibility that immediately comes to the forefront is that Jesus sought to demonstrate through this parable the greatness of God's love and his willingness to forgive. Throughout the history of the church the parable has been interpreted as teaching this as its main point, and we shall see that the parable does portray in a most vivid way the graciousness of God. If the parable had originally ended at 15:24, then indeed we would have to conclude that the point of the parable in the *Sitz im Leben* of Jesus was to proclaim the love and mercy of God and his joy in forgiving sinners. This would also fit in well with the theme of the preceding two parables which speak of the "joy before the angels of God over one sinner who repents" (15:10; cf. also 15:7). Yet the parable consists of two parts and has three main characters: the younger son, the older son, and the father. Of these the only character who shares the forefront in both halves of the parable is the father. He, rather than the prodigal or his older brother, is therefore the main character. As a result, the parable is misnamed when it is entitled "the parable of the prodigal son" because the title does not focus on the main character—the father—and it ignores the second part of the parable. A far better heading would appear to be "the parable of the gracious father."

As we seek to arrive at the main point of this parable for the *Sitz im Leben* of Jesus, we must identify the audience to which Jesus directed this parable. Luke 15:1-2 states that the parable was addressed to the Pharisees and scribes in response to their question of why Jesus associated with publicans and sinners. That these two verses were written by Luke as an introduction for the following three parables seems clear.[24] Nevertheless it seems reasonable to conclude that Luke 15:1-2 is an accurate portrayal of the situation in which this parable was originally uttered, in the light of the second half of the parable. It is in this section that we find the main emphasis of Jesus. The rule of end stress should cause us to focus our attention on the last confrontation of the father and the older son rather than on the first encounter of the father and the younger son. In the parable Jesus does not seek primarily to assure "prodigals" that God loves them and is gracious, although the parable certainly teaches this. Rather he seeks to defend before the Pharisees and scribes God's gracious offer of salvation to prodigals and the wrongness of their opposition to his ministry.[25]

> The parable of the Prodigal Son is . . . not primarily a proclama-
> tion of the Good News to the poor, but a vindication of the Good
> News in reply to its critics. Jesus' justification lies in the boundless
> love of God.[26]

In the light of the first *Sitz im Leben* it is therefore evident that the audience to which Jesus addressed this parable needed to be rebuked as to their negative attitude toward Jesus' offer of the kingdom of God to the outcasts. Why, then, have we dealt with this parable in a chapter concerned with a description of the God of Jesus' parables? The reason is clear, for while it is true that the main emphasis of Jesus in this parable is aimed not at describing the loving character of God, the fact remains that the description of the goodness of God is integral to the parable. The character of God, described by the actions of the father in the parable, is integral to Jesus' main point. It is precisely this kind of God that Jesus' critics cannot envision. To use this parable therefore to describe the character of God is not to err in pressing details! The main point involves the character of God as portrayed by the father and the stumbling block this God is for the Pharisees and scribes.

The parable teaches in beautiful simplicity what God is like, his limitless love, his boundless love, his amazing grace. In Jesus' ministry God has come in grace offering forgiveness and pardon to outcasts as well as to "righteous." The kingdom of God has come, and all are invited to share. Now is the acceptable time (2 Cor 6:2). The acceptable year of the Lord has dawned in which good news comes to the poor, captives are released, the blind receive their sight, and the oppressed are set free (Luke 4:18-19). Yet the God of the parables is also a God of righteousness and holiness. As we shall see in the next chapter, judgment is coming. It already is now casting its shadow on the earth.

But still there is time. God in his mercy offers salvation to all. No one need despair—not even the publicans and sinners!

The Interpretation of the Parable by the Evangelist

In order to understand how Luke used this parable in his Gospel, we can obtain greater benefit by observing how the parable fits the general Lukan scheme than by seeking to isolate particular terms or expressions that the Evangelist may have added to the parable. The parable clearly fits well the Lukan emphasis on salvation[27] and in particular his emphasis on the need of repentance. The vocabulary, redaction, and selection of material by Luke clearly reveals this emphasis. In Luke the terms "repentance" (*metanoia*), "to repent" (*metanoeō*), and "to turn/repent" (*epistrephō*) are used a total of seventeen times, whereas in Matthew and Mark they are used only seven and four times respectively.[28] Luke also contains seven stories dealing with sin and repentance and five of these are only found in Luke (Luke 5:1-11; 7:36-50; 15:11-32; 19:1-10; 23:39-41; and LUKE 5:17-26; 22:31-34, 61). It is furthermore in Luke where we read that "the Son of man came to seek and to save the lost" (19:10), and it is Luke who in his redaction adds to MARK 2:17 ("I came not to call the righteous, but sinners") the expression "to repentance."

It is evident from the above that a key, if not the key, emphasis in Luke-Acts is the call to repentance and the offer of salvation to all. We have previously pointed out the Lukan emphasis on God's grace being extended to the outcasts of society, i.e., the lost.[29] The parable of the gracious father certainly fits this theme well.[30] In this we find a great similarity between the concerns of Jesus in the first *Sitz im Leben* and that of Luke in the third.

ADDITIONAL PARABLE DEMONSTRATING THE GRACIOUSNESS OF GOD

Another passage quite similar to the parable of the gracious father is the parable of the laborers of the vineyard or, as it is more appropriately called, the parable of the gracious employer.

The Gracious Employer (Matt 20:1-16)

For the kingdom of heaven is like a householder who went out early in the morning to hire laborers for his vineyard. After agreeing with the laborers for a denarius a day, he sent them into his vineyard. And going out about the third hour he saw others standing idle in the market place; and to them he said, "You go into the vineyard too, and whatever is right I will give you." So they went. Going out again about the sixth hour and the ninth hour, he did the same. And about the eleventh hour he went out and found others standing; and he said to them, "Why do you stand here idle all day?" They said to him, "Because no one has hired us." He said to them, "You go into the vineyard too." And when evening came, the owner of the vineyard said to his steward, "Call the laborers and pay them their wages, beginning with the last, up to the first." And when those hired about the eleventh hour came, each of them received a denarius. Now when the first came, they thought they would receive more; but each of them also received a denarius. And on receiving it they grumbled at the householder, saying, "These last worked only one hour, and you have made them equal to us who have borne the burden of the day and the scorching heat." But he replied to one of them, "Friend, I am doing you no wrong; did you not agree with me for a denarius? Take what belongs to you, and go; I choose to give to this last as I give to you. Am I not allowed to do what I choose with what belongs to me? Or do you begrudge my generosity?" So the last will be first, and the first last. (Matt 20:1-16)

In our parable the owner of a vineyard ("householder," RSV) seeks the employment of workers in his vineyard. He proceeds out early in the morning (6 A.M.) and upon agreement of a denarius hires men to work a twelve-hour day in his vineyard. He goes out again in the third (9 A.M.), the sixth (12 A.M.), the ninth (3 P.M.), and the eleventh hour (5 P.M.) and hires more. It has been suggested that the frequent traveling of the owner to the marketplace in order to hire workers reveals that he found himself in a critical emergency. Some have even suggested that his grape harvest was at a critical point and that the next day was the sabbath.[31] We do not find in the parable itself, however, any clear evidence of such an emergency, and we should probably therefore not read into the parable a pressing harvest situation.[32] This is especially so since the treatment by the owner of those who worked only one hour is seen as an act of generosity and goodness and not recompense for helping the owner out in his time of need. When the end of the day comes, in accordance with the Law (Lev 19:13; Deut 24:14-15.), the workers are paid beginning with those hired last to those hired first. To the amazement and frustration of the earliest workers, all are paid the same wage—one denarius.[33] In response the earliest workers grumble and rudely (note the omission of a title of address to the owner) claim that they have been wronged since they had indeed labored much harder and longer than the last workers and yet had received the same amount. To this the owner makes a threefold defense: (1) no injustice has been done them, for they had received the agreed-upon wage (v. 13b-c);[34] (2) he has the right to do what he wants with his own possessions, especially when he is showing generosity in his use of them (v. 14); and (3) the basic issue is not that they have been wronged but that they are jealous (literally, they have an evil eye) that others have been treated generously. The parable then ends with a general proverb about the last being first and the first last.

One cannot help being impressed once again by the artistry with which this parable is told. The beautiful staging must be observed. Although the order of hiring is, of course, from the earliest to the latest, the payment of the wages is in reverse order. As a result we have a heightening of expectation on the part of the earliest workers.[35] The presence of the householder at the end of the day is also unusual, since it was the steward's function to distribute the wages at the end of the day. Yet the presence of the owner is needed for the dialogue to follow. Finally, in the conclusion of the parable the paying of the third-, sixth-, and ninth-hour workers is simply eliminated since they are unimportant for the point of the parable.[36]

Of all the parables of Jesus this may well be one of the most vexing and irritating of all for present-day readers. More often than not the reader finds himself identifying and sympathizing with the first workers, for one's sense of justice seems to support their claim that they should have received more than the last workers. Even when it is granted that the parable should not be pressed as an example of ideal labor-management relations (for what union official would dare agree to such a wage agreement?), the parable is nonetheless a stumbling block to one's sense of right and wrong. All this, we shall see, indicates that even though as Christians we seek to follow the teachings of Jesus with all our heart, mind, and soul, we still have more of a "Pharisaic heart" within us than we frequently realize.

What, then, is the point of the parable? It is clear today that the attempt by the early church to see in the parable a portrayal of the history of salvation is an error. Yet several other possibilities do present themselves. Is the point of the parable that God is sovereign and can do whatever he wills (v. 15)? Surely this is to read into the parable something that is not there, for whereas the owner can "sovereignly" give more to the last workers than they deserve, he cannot sovereignly withhold or give less than the denarius to the first workers! A more likely possibility is that Jesus in the parable seeks to demonstrate that salvation is by grace alone. This interpretation has had a continual succession of proponents since the time of Luther.[37] Yet not only does this look like a reading of this basic Reformation issue into the parable, it is refuted by the fact that the first workers clearly earned their denarius or "salvation." Are we to conclude that some people are saved by grace alone (eleventh hour); some people completely earn their salvation on an agreed-upon basis (first workers); and others obtain their salvation by various combinations of works and grace (third, sixth, and ninth hours)? This is clearly not a correct interpretation of the parable.[38]

Another possible interpretation of the parable is that it seeks to demonstrate the mercy of God. To be sure, the parable does teach this, but here again as in the parable of the gracious father (Luke 15:11–32), if this were the main point, the conclusion of the parable would be unnecessary.[39] The grumbling of the first workers would furthermore not only be unnecessary, but actually detract from this point by taking our eyes off the eleventh-hour workers and focusing upon the earliest workers. Finally, it should be pointed out that if this were the main point, then the laborers would have been paid in the order of employment, so that the acts of graciousness toward the poor would come at the end of the parable and receive the end stress. The rule of end stress would indicate that the point of this parable lies in the interaction of the owner and the grumbling first workers. When one takes note of the ending of this parable, one cannot help noting that this parable is almost a carbon copy of the parable of the gracious father. In both we have a conclusion in which faithful people (first workers and older brother) grumble/are angry at the gracious goodness of the owner/father in blessing the last workers/younger brother. In the *Sitz im Leben* of Jesus this parable was almost certainly addressed to those who opposed Jesus' offer of God's mercy and grace to the poor and outcasts. Only in interpreting the parable in this manner does the picture part (the grumbling of the first workers over the graciousness shown by the owner to the last workers) and the proposed reality part (the grumbling of the Pharisees and scribes over the gracious offer by God of his kingdom to publicans and sinners) coalesce satisfactorily.

Again we see in this parable a description of the gracious character of God as portrayed by the owner of the vineyard. God is good, i.e., generous (Matt 20:15). His goodness and grace are such that we are simply incapable of accepting it. Our lack of perfect "goodness" is offended by the parable, and we identify with the first workers all too easily. Yet if we were truly good and loving, even if we were the first workers, would we not as good people rather than grumbling reply something like, "Is it not wonderful that those who worked only an hour also received a denarius as we did?" And would we not rejoice with them? Jeremias points out that Jesus in the parable wanted to show the Pharisees and scribes how unjustified, hateful, loveless, and unmerciful their criticism really was.[40] It is frightening to realize that our identification with the first workers, and hence with the opponents of Jesus, reveals how loveless and unmerciful we basically are. We may be more "under law" in our thinking and less "under grace" than we realize. God is good and compassionate far beyond his children's understanding!

One final issue that must be dealt with in this parable is the concluding statement: "So the last will be first, and the first last." The general consensus among New Testament scholars is that this was not originally part of the parable but is a conclusion that has been added later.[41] The saying itself may have been an independent proverb going back to Jesus (cf. LUKE 13:30; MARK 10:31), but it was placed at this point by Matthew, due to Matt 20:8b, "Call the laborers and pay them their wages, beginning with the last, up to the first." If, on the other hand, the placement of the proverb is pre-Matthean, this would explain why Matthew located the parable here in his Gospel, for since the story of the rich young ruler ended with, "But many that are first will be last, and the last first," Matthew may have added this parable with its similar ending at this point.[42] The appropriateness of this conclusion for the parable is almost universally denied on the basis that the parable does not speak of any reversal of rank or privilege as implied in the saying.[43] Yet there is a sense in which this conclusion does "fit" the parable. If the proposed *Sitz im Leben* of the parable is indeed Jesus' defense of his association with publicans and sinners and his offering to them the kingdom of God, then there is a sense in which the parable does reveal that "the last will be first, and the first last." In the context which Jesus told this parable is it not true that the last (the publicans and sinners) are indeed the first to accept the offer of the kingdom of God, whereas the first (the religious elite—the Pharisees and scribes) are the last to accept it? It may therefore be premature to conclude that the closing proverb does not fit the parable. True, it does not fit the story of the parable itself, but it does fit quite well the broader context in which Jesus told the parable and in which a true reversal of roles is taking place, and elsewhere Jesus explicitly refers to this reversal (Luke 7:29-30; Matt 21:31c).[44]

CONCLUSION

In our discussion of the parables of the gracious father and the gracious employer we have seen that the character of God portrayed in them is one of grace and mercy. Elsewhere in the parables we also see this portrayal of God. He is one who in mercy forgives great sins, even the sins of a prostitute (Luke 7:41-43, the two debtors);[45] he is not merely content to forgive those who come to him but seeks out the lost to show his mercy (LUKE 15:4-7, the lost sheep); whereas he despises the boastful and the proud, he justifies the unjust, adulterers, and tax collectors who humbly seek his mercy (Luke 18:9-14, the Pharisee and the publican). How gracious is the God of the parables. Even in the depths of man's worst sin, he reaches out in mercy and forgiveness. No one need despair. Tax collectors, prodigals, and sinners of all description can return to the God of the parables, and this God does not merely wait for them to return, he seeks after them. The Hound of Heaven[46] seeks out the lost in order to bestow his mercy upon them. Dare the church teach, however, that no matter how badly we sin we should always remember that God longs for us and will always accept us? Is this not a dangerous teaching? Perhaps, but so is the entire New Testament teaching of justification by faith.[47] The God of the parables would impress on all the knowledge that he is gracious and delights in forgiveness. Only if we remember this, can we ever "come to ourselves" (Luke 15:16) and return to our Creator and be forgiven.

> But thou, O Lord, art a God merciful and gracious,
>> slow to anger and abounding in steadfast love and faithfulness.
>>> (Ps 86:15)

CHAPTER 10

THE FINAL JUDGMENT

THE KINGDOM OF GOD has come in the ministry of Jesus, and with this goes out the call to decision. God in his grace and mercy is seeking out the lost and longs to make them his sons and daughters. Now is the day of salvation! Now is the time of mercy in which all people are urged to "Seek the LORD while he may be found, call upon him while he is near" (Isa 55:6), for there is another day coming of which the parables also speak. "In that day" the God of grace will judge the world in holiness and righteousness. The following is one passage in which this final judgment is portrayed by Jesus.

THE PARABLE OF THE SHEEP AND THE GOATS (MATT 25:31-46)

When the Son of man comes in his glory, and all the angels with him, then he will sit on his glorious throne. Before him will be gathered all the nations, and he will separate them one from another as a shepherd separates the sheep from the goats, and he will place the sheep at his right hand, but the goats at the left. Then the King will say to those at his right hand, "Come, O blessed of my Father, inherit the kingdom prepared for you from the foundation of the world; for I was hungry and you gave me food, I was thirsty and you gave me drink, I was a stranger and you welcomed me, I was naked and you clothed me, I was sick and you visited me, I was in prison and you came to me." Then the righteous will answer him, "Lord, when did we see thee hungry and feed thee, or thirsty and give thee drink? And when did we see thee a stranger and welcome thee, or naked and clothe thee? And when did we see thee sick or in prison and visit thee?" And the King will answer them, "Truly, I say to you, as you did it to one of the least of these my brethren, you did it to me." Then he will say

> to those at his left hand, "Depart from me, you cursed, into the
> eternal fire prepared for the devil and his angels; for I was hungry
> and you gave me no food, I was thirsty and you gave me no drink,
> I was a stranger and you did not welcome me, naked and you did
> not clothe me, sick and in prison and you did not visit me." Then
> they also will answer, "Lord, when did we see thee hungry or
> thirsty or a stranger or naked or sick or in prison, and did not
> minister to thee?" Then he will answer them, "Truly, I say to you,
> as you did it not to one of the least of these, you did it not to me."
> And they will go away into eternal punishment, but the righteous
> into eternal life. (Matt 25:31-46)

Is the above properly called "a parable"? Strictly speaking the only pure parabolic element in the passage is found in vs. 32-33 where we have the similitude of the shepherd separating the sheep from the goats. Yet the entire passage contains much figurative language and is certainly a word picture of the final judgment,[1] and in most works on the subject the passage is treated as a parable.[2] For these reasons we shall therefore discuss the entire passage as a "parable" of the final judgment.

Our passage raises a number of questions at the very beginning. Some of these involve questions of authenticity such as: Are the references to the "Son of man" and the description of the Son of man as "King" authentic? Is the entire passage a Matthean creation? Is it a pre-Matthean creation? Or is it for the most part authentic? Other key questions that arise might be: Are the people who are judged Gentiles, Gentiles and Jews, or Christians and non-Christians? Are those described as "the least of these my brethren" needy people in general, the Christian community, or Christian missionaries? Finally we should note that the passage distinguishes between two groups of the elect: the "sheep" and "the least of these my brethren." How can sense be made of this? We shall not deal with all these questions at this time, but in the course of our discussion we shall have to discuss each of them.

Perhaps the most serious arguments against the authenticity of the Son of man designation in our passage is that the function of the Son of man has changed from that of witnessing to judging and the fact that it is in Matthew alone that the Son of man is portrayed as sitting on a throne (cf. Matt 19:28). While it is true that the portrayal of the Son of man sitting upon the throne comes either from the M material or from Matthew's own redaction, the portrayal of the Son of man in the role of judge is clearly pre-Matthean. The warning to watch in Luke 21:36 is given in order that the believer will be able "to stand before the Son of man," and clearly the Son of man is acting here as a judge (cf. MARK 8:38). It is also evident that by his very coming the Son of man will bring judgment to the world in his gathering (separating) his own from the world (MARK 13:27; MATT 24:27). It is therefore incorrect to claim that outside of Matt 25:31f. the Son of man is not portrayed in a judging function. It must furthermore be asked how judgment can ever be separated from the role of the Son of man since the Old Testament background of this title refers to his receiving everlasting dominion over all peoples, nations, and languages (Dan 7:13-14). Enoch also portrays the Son of man in a judgment role.[3] There does not seem, therefore, to be a serious problem with regard to the authenticity of the portrayal of the Son of man functioning as a judge. On the contrary, it is hard to envision the Son of man apart from some judgmental role and function.

A similar problem involves the portrayal of the Son of man as "King" (Matt 25:34, 40). It has been argued that such a portrayal is contrary both to the pre-Matthean tradition and to the teachings of Jesus. Again, however, one must take note of the Old Testament background for the Son of man title. In Dan 7:13-14 the Son of man is given "dominion" and his "kingdom" is referred to. Can one have dominion over all peoples, nations, and languages and possess a kingdom without being a "king"? Surely the Son of man of Dan 7:13-14 is a king! The Son of man of Enoch 62:5 (cf. also 51:3 and 55:4) is likewise portrayed as sitting on the throne of his glory. Here, too, we see in this Son of man figure a king of some sort, for the presence of a throne demands such an understanding. We find a similar portrayal of the Son of man in LUKE 22:28-30. If Matt 25:31-46 did not use the term "King" in vs. 34 and 40, would we not, because of the reference to the Son of man's coming in glory and his being seated on a throne, need to assume that he is a king? If vs. 34 and 40 had "referred to 'the judge,' no one would have batted an eyelid. But to blink at the term 'king' is to presume quite inaccurately some difference between the two."[4] There is therefore no necessity for assuming that the portrayal of the Son of man in the role of king must be attributed to Matthew's redactional work. On the contrary it may very well be that we find in this portrayal the teaching of Jesus himself.[5]

To argue that the portrayal of the Son of man as judge and king in our passage does not come from Matthew does not mean, of course, that this passage has not undergone editorial work at the hand of the Evangelist. It is evident from a careful analysis of the passage that we find in a number of instances the redactional activity of the Evangelist.

The description found in v. 31 does correspond closely to similar descriptions in 16:27 and 19:28 and thus leads one to believe that Matthew may have reworked the introduction of the passage using his own terminology. This is also true of such expressions as "my Father" (v. 34), which occurs some sixteen times in Matthew but only four times in Luke and not once in Mark, the frequent use of "then" (vs. 31, 34, 37, 41, 44, 45), which occurs nearly ninety times in Matthew but only fifteen times in Luke and six times in Mark, etc. The theme of judgment in this passage is also a Matthean emphasis.[6] As a result of the clear evidence of Matthew's redactional work, some scholars have denied the authenticity of the entire passage.[7] Yet such a conclusion would appear overly negative. It seems rather that "despite evidences of Matthean stylization, the parable is substantially genuine."[8] Whereas the pre-Matthean nucleus of the passage is most clearly seen in vs. 32-33c and 42-45,[9] it is probable that the Son of man title in v. 31 is also authentic, and that there is no need to see any conflict between this title and the title "King" in v. 40 since the "glorious throne" of v. 31 already refers to the kingship of the Son of man.

The Historical Setting of the Parable

Our passage is a picturesque portrayal of the final judgment. The scene is in no way new or unique to Jesus, for it is, to use Old Testament terminology, a description of "the day of the Lord."[10] All nations are gathered before the Son of man, for judgment is to be given (v. 32). The scene is not that of a trial, for no defense is possible. Excuses are worthless; it is time for judgment! All that remains is the sentencing. "All the nations" are gathered for this judgment. In Joel 3:11f. and Enoch 62-63 a distinction is drawn between the judgment of the nations and the judgment of Israel. Does Matt 25:31-46 presuppose a similar distinction? In Matthew the expression "all the nations" is found five times. In at least two instances it is clear that the expression includes both Jews and Gentiles, for in 24:14 the gospel is to be preached "throughout the whole world, as a testimony to all nations" and it is difficult to exclude the Jews from this statement. Also in 28:19 Jesus commissions his disciples to "make disciples of all nations" because he now has all authority in heaven and on earth. Here again it is difficult to read into this reference to "all nations" the exclusion of the Jews.[11] With regard to the latter Luke 24:47 (and Acts 1:8) is in full agreement, for the command to preach the gospel "to all nations" is to begin in Jerusalem! For Matthew it is clear that the judgment scene includes in the expression "all nations" both Jew and Gentile, but was this true for Jesus as well? There is no reason to think that Jesus excluded the Jew from this expression, for certainly he taught that judgment was coming upon Judaism. Had he not warned Chorazin and Bethsaida about the day of judgment (MATT 11:21)? And surely the woes of Luke 6:24-26 were warnings to his fellow Jews of the judgment to come. The apocalypse of Mark 13 likewise cannot be read without the awareness that Israel, too, will be judged. Like Amos and John the Baptist before him, Jesus warned that the day of the Lord brought to Jew as well as Gentile darkness and not light, gloom and not brightness (Amos 5:18-20), unless they repented. It is difficult, therefore, to envision Jesus portraying the final judgment of all nations and excluding the Jews from that judgment. Ultimately all humanity fell into two categories—those who were the children of the kingdom (whether Jew or Gentile) and those who were not (whether Jew or Gentile).

The judgment itself is portrayed by the parable of the shepherd separating his flock. This was a familiar scene in Palestine, for mixed flocks were common, and whereas the sheep preferred the open air and could be left safely in the pastures at night, the goats were more susceptible to the cold and had to be kept warm and, if possible, sheltered. Since the term "sheep" is frequently used in the Old Testament as a metaphor for the people of God and since sheep were more valuable than goats, the "blessed" are designated in the passage by this metaphor whereas the "cursed" are designated by the metaphor of "the goats." The male goats' tendency to be more wild than their counterparts in the sheep may also be relevant for the metaphor. The judgment is described as separating the "blessed" to the right and the "cursed" to the left, for the "right" is frequently linked to what is favorable and good in the Old Testament, whereas the "left" is associated with negative values.[12]

The basis for this blessedness comes as a complete surprise to the "sheep." Without their knowing, they have ministered to Jesus in the form of caring for his brethren. This caring is described by means of six works of love: feeding the hungry; giving drink to the thirsty; offering hospitality to the stranger; clothing the naked; visiting the sick; and visiting those in prison. The importance of these works of love is witnessed to by the fact that they are repeated four times in the passage (vs. 35-36, 37-39, 42-43, 44). What is surprising to the sheep, however, is that they performed these acts of love, the king says, to him! When the sheep in amazement inquire how this took place (vs. 37-39), they are then told that when they performed these acts to even the least of his brethren they did it to him. It is interesting to note that whereas today's readers tend to ask, "How can these things be?" there is no such question raised by the "sheep" and the "goats." They understood this concept of corporate personality or solidarity.[13] They knew that a man's envoy or representative is as himself,[14] so that the way one treats the brethren is in effect the way one is treating the king they represent. Elsewhere Jesus teaches this same concept when he says:

> He who receives you receives me, and he who receives me receives him who sent me. . . . And whoever gives to one of these little ones even a cup of cold water because he is a disciple, truly, I say to you, he shall not lose his reward. (Matt 10:40, 42)[15]

Unfortunately the "cursed" are reminded that not having performed these acts of love to the brethren means that they did not perform them to the king as well.[16] The cause of their condemnation is not due to their having performed great evil but rather due to their not having performed the loving acts which they ought to have done. The parable of the rich man and Lazarus (Luke 16:19-31) is another good example of this principle. The rich man did not actively harm Lazarus. His sin was that he did not do any positive good to him! For Jesus, the negative golden rule of Tobit 4:15 ("And what you hate, do not do to any one") is not enough. We must love our neighbors as ourselves and this involves doing acts of love. A sound tree bears good fruit (MATT 7:17), and in that day the sheep and the goats will be known by their fruit (MATT 7:20).

The Point of the Parable in the First Sitz im Leben

For many this passage appears to conflict with the teaching found elsewhere in the Bible, especially in Paul, that one's standing before God in the final day is not dependent on "works" but on faith and that it is through faith alone that one's name is written in the Book of Life. Does this passage conflict with the Reformation's emphasis on justification by faith? It should be pointed out that even Paul, who taught, "And to one who does not work but trusts him who justifies the ungodly, his faith is reckoned as righteousness" (Rom 4:5), says explicitly, "For in Christ Jesus neither circumcision nor uncircumcision is of any avail, but faith working through love" (Gal 5:6), and, "For it is not the hearers of the law who are righteous before God, but the doers of the law who will be justified" (Rom 2:13). The biblical teaching is clear. We are saved by faith alone, but the kind of faith that saves is never alone. Saving faith is faith that works through love. Whereas Paul in his debates with the Judaizers needed to emphasize that salvation is by grace through faith in order to refute the notion that somehow by one's works one can merit acceptance with God,[17] Jesus in this parable emphasized the issue of how one can know if someone has such faith. By their fruit, i.e., by the presence or absence of these six works of love, the King will judge whether one has a true "faith working through love."

That behind these activities there lies a true faith (or lack of faith when these works of love are not present) is evident for at least two reasons. For one, these acts of love are extended to the "brethren" and this along with the kind of love portrayed reveals that the "brethren" are best understood as being either Christians or more probably Christian missionaries,[18] and generally one's response to the Christian or Christian missionary is at the same time a response to the Christian message. Mark 9:41 supports this view, for there Jesus says, "For truly, I say to you, whoever gives you a cup of water to drink because you bear the name of Christ, will by no means lose his reward." Secondly, it should be noted that there is no middle ground in the parable or in Jesus' teachings. One either inherits the kingdom or departs into the eternal fire. There is no neutral state. Yet the degree of loving acts which are or are not performed to others does not provide a sure basis for such an absolute division. Faith in or commitment to the King, however, does. One is either for or against Christ (Luke 11:23). Acceptance or rejection are absolutes here. Thus it seems most reasonable to assume that lying beneath the performance or omission of these acts of love is the ultimate cause of faith or lack of faith.[19] That faith, if it is true faith, can be recognized by the love it produces.

We need now to draw some conclusions as to what the main point of the parable was in the *Sitz im Leben* of Jesus. Clearly that point centers around the theme of a final irrevocable judgment, and with this Jesus' audience would wholeheartedly have agreed. That such a view was a given for most Jews is evident from Paul's argument in Rom 3:5-8. Here Paul refutes the argument that God is unjust by pointing out that if this were true, he could not judge the world (Rom 3:6), but since we know as a fact that God will judge the world, he must therefore be just! The basis of this judgment, however, differed for Jesus and his opponents. The basis of judgment was not due to loyalty to the law, as legalistically understood by some Pharisees, but rather due to the doing (or not doing) deeds of mercy to the "brethren" (Matt 25:40).

Who then are these "brethren"? And who are the "nations" and the "sheep"? At this point we shall have to anticipate our discussion of the passage in the context of the *Sitz im Leben* of the Evangelist, but for Jesus as well as for Matthew it would appear that the final judgment of all nations (Jew and Gentiles) is seen as based upon the response that they give to the messengers of Jesus, i.e., the "brethren," in their proclamation of Jesus' message. This response is portrayed not so much from the aspect of whether they believe in Jesus Christ but whether they possess a life-changing belief which produces acts of love to the messengers of Jesus.

The Interpretation of the Parable by the Evangelist

Although reference has been made as to who the "brethren" of v. 40 are, discussion of this question has been withheld up to this point. In the present state of the passage, to whom does this designation refer? Jeremias has argued that the expression refers to all the poor and needy of the world,[20] but there are many reasons for understanding the expression as referring primarily to the disciples. The term itself must first be investigated. That the term was a common designation for Christians is evident,[21] so that Matthew and his readers would probably have understood this designation as a reference to their fellow Christians, unless there was sufficient reason for not doing so. In only two other places in Matthew is the expression "my brethren" found, and in both instances it refers to fellow Christians and especially to the disciples.

> And stretching out his hand toward his disciples, he said, "Here are my mother and my brothers! For whoever does the will of my Father in heaven is my brother, and sister, and mother." (Matt 12:49-50; Matthew here is using MARK 3:34-35)

> So they departed quickly from the tomb with fear and great joy, and ran to tell his disciples. . . . Then Jesus said to them, "Do not be afraid; go and tell my brethren to go to Galilee, and there they will see me." (Matt 28:8, 10)[22]

Secondly, it should be observed that the best passage available for understanding Matt 25:40 is Matt 10:40-42. Here we read:

> He who receives you receives me and he who receives me receives him who sent me. He who receives a prophet because he is a prophet shall receive a prophet's reward, and he who receives a righteous man because he is a righteous man shall receive a righteous man's reward. And whoever gives to one of these little

ones even a cup of cold water because he is a disciple, truly, I say to
you, he shall not lose his reward. (Matt 10:40-42)

The parallelism between this passage and our parable should be
carefully observed: "little ones" (10:42) = "least of these" (25:40);
"receives you receives me" (10:40) = "as you did it to one of the least of
these my brethren, you did it to me" (25:40); "cold water"
(10:42) = "gave thee drink" (25:35, 37).[23] Finally it should be pointed out
that if the "brethren" are interpreted as referring to the poor and needy
of the world, how are they then to be distinguished from the nations
being judged? If the "brethren," however, are interpreted as referring
to the disciples and missionaries, then such a distinction makes good
sense. This would mean that the "redeemed" are portrayed as
consisting of two groups—the "sheep" and the "brethren"—and this
portrayal of the redeemed into two groups is what we find in Matt
10:40-42 as well. There we read of the "little ones" and those who
receive reward for their treatment of these "little ones." The term
"brethren" is then best understood as referring to the disciples or
Christian missionaries who proclaim the message of the kingdom, and
the "sheep" are those among the nations who respond in faith to the
Christian message and whose "newness of life" (Rom 6:4) results in
acts of love. The "goats," on the other hand, are those among the
nations who do not respond in faith and do not live lives filled with acts
of love. The Book of Acts provides us a good example of the behavior of
the sheep in the account of the Philippian jailer who, upon believing
the gospel preached by Paul and Silas, performed acts of love toward
them (Acts 16:30-34). A negative example is provided by Matthew in
10:14-15 where during the ministry of Jesus the messengers that he is
sending out are told to shake off the dust from their feet as they leave
the houses or towns of those who do not receive them or listen to their
words. It should be remembered that this last example is found in the
Gospel of Matthew itself, so that it would appear that for Matthew at
least the parable teaches that the reception of the Christian
missionaries (and the message they bring) will be the decisive factor by
which the nations will be judged on the final day. For Jew and Gentile
alike the decisive issue is what they will do with the message of Jesus
and this will be most manifest by their treatment of these messengers.
The Son of man has received "all authority in heaven and on earth"
(Matt 28:18). He is King! And he will render judgment. The rejection of
his gracious offer of forgiveness will bring disaster for the goats but the
acceptance of his grace will bring for the sheep life everlasting.

The question must now be raised as to whether this interpretation of the passage by Matthew is essentially the same as that of Jesus or whether it stands in opposition to Jesus' own teaching. One objection to the view that the "brethren" refer to the disciples or Christian missionaries is that this "would be to assume a world-wide mission to the remotest nations, a conception which does not correspond with the outlook of Jesus."[24] There are a number of issues which must be raised, however, with regard to this objection. For one, it must be asked how we can be so sure that the historical Jesus never envisioned some sort of mission among the Gentiles. If Matt 10:5-6 is raised in support of this view, it need only be pointed out that at other times and in other places Jesus did go and preach on non-Jewish soil (cf. MARK 7:24 to 9:1 and Luke 9:51-56).

Of particular relevance to this question is the fact that the Gospels record a number of instances in which the disciples were sent out to preach the good news of the kingdom of God. In MARK 6:6-11 we have a pre-Easter tradition of Jesus sending out (literally, *apostellein*) the disciples to preach, and it is clear that judgment is forthcoming if they are not given food and drink or are not welcomed. We therefore have in the *Sitz im Leben* of Jesus a clear instance where such missionary teaching fits well.[25] In LUKE 10:1-12 we have an additional sending out of the Seventy, and here we find that those who welcome the messengers and give them food and drink are expressly blessed with "peace" (v. 6), whereas those who do not receive them are warned that judgment awaits them by the parabolic action of the messengers shaking the dust off their feet (v. 11). It will be better for such a wicked city as Sodom (v. 12) in the final judgment than for those cities which reject the messengers of Jesus. It is quite probable that Luke has edited this tradition available to him and shaped it for use in the ongoing mission of the church of his day. And in a similar way it is quite probable that Matthew has done the same with regard to Matt 25:31-46, but there is no need to assume that both traditions are *de novo* creations of the early church. On the contrary it is difficult to believe that Jesus did not send out his disciples to preach, and that this was one of his purposes in choosing the Twelve is expressly stated in MARK 3:14. It is also probable that Jesus recognized that one's reception of a messenger is in fact one's reception of the one represented, so that such sayings as Matt 10:40 ("He who receives you receives me") (cf. also Mark 9:37; Luke 10:16; John 12:44; 13:20) indicate that such ideas as found in Matt 25:35-36, 40, 42-43 fit well the ministry of Jesus. It would appear therefore that whereas certain editorial reworking by Matthew of Matt 25:31-46 must be acknowledged, there is no need to see any substantial difference between the main point of the parable in the first *Sitz im Leben* and in the third.

Additional Parables of Judgment

Two additional and much debated parables dealing with the theme of judgment are the parable of the wheat and the tares and the parable of the great net.

The Great Net (Matt 13:47-50)

> Again, the kingdom of heaven is like a net which was thrown into the sea and gathered fish of every kind; when it was full, men drew it ashore and sat down and sorted the good into vessels but threw away the bad. So it will be at the close of the age. The angels will come out and separate the evil from the righteous, and throw them into the furnace of fire; there men will weep and gnash their teeth. (Matt 13:47-50)

In this parable the kingdom of God is likened not to a great net that catches good and bad fish but rather to the entire activity of netting, catching, and sorting portrayed in the parable.[26] The scene portrayed in this parable is that of a large seine net which is passing through the sea (no doubt the Sea of Galilee) in order to catch fish.[27] This could be done in several ways. The net could be stretched out between two boats which then headed for shore. Then the net, buoyed up at the top by floats and weighted at the bottom, would be dragged ashore. Sometimes a single boat could also be used and could either stretch out the net, which would then be dragged to the shore by men standing on the shore, or else one end of the net could be tied to the shore and the boat would make a large semicircle sweeping all in its path to shore. After the net was dragged ashore, the good fish (those ceremonially clean) were kept and placed in a basket and the bad (those ceremonially unclean and thus forbidden for consumption) were then thrown away on the shore to rot.

After the picture part of the parable, there comes an interpretation in which the separation of the good fish from the bad fish is likened to the final judgment when there will be a separation of the righteous from the evil and the latter are thrown "into the furnace of fire." As in the case of the other interpretations of the parables found in the Gospels, the authenticity of this interpretation has been challenged and denied. At times the interpretation is rejected *a priori* on the grounds that since all parables are self-evident, they do not require an interpretation.[28] The error of this premise is more readily acknowledged today.[29] Furthermore the very fact that so many parables in the Gospels have interpretations attributed to Jesus[30] should make us cautious in making such a statement, for whereas one might be able to argue for the possibility or even the probability that any canonical interpretation of the parables is inauthentic, the probability of every single one being inauthentic would appear to be rather small. If an interpretation of a parable fits the *Sitz im Leben* of Jesus, there is no necessity for looking elsewhere for a source, and even those interpretations which fit a post-resurrection setting better than a pre-resurrection one may not necessarily be *de novo* creations by the Evangelist or the early church but rather may be modifications of a dominical interpretation made to fit the new *Sitz im Leben* of the church.

In looking at the interpretation of this parable, we discover reasons that have been advanced as to why the present interpretation may be the interpretation of the Evangelist rather than that of Jesus. One argument is that v. 49 does not portray the final judgment of the world but rather the judgment of the church, and this demands a post-resurrection setting. Yet the expression "from [literally, out of the midst of] the righteous" cannot all by itself require that the interpretation must be understood as portraying the judgment of the professing church. It could be understood as a separation of the evil from the righteous in the world. In its present location in Matthew the parable is addressed to the disciples (see 13:36),[31] but to say that the parable is restricted therefore even in its Matthean setting to the judgment of the church alone seems to go too far. One argument sometimes used to limit the judgment portrayed in the parable to the church is the fact that the net does not sweep into it all the fish of the sea but only a portion of them. Yet surely this is to ask too much of any comparison. Many times Jesus used limited analogies to describe a universal truth. The kingdom of God is likened, for instance, to *some* leaven, *a* grain of mustard seed, seed falling upon *one* farmer's field, *ten* maidens, etc. Another argument raised against the authenticity of the interpretation is that it supposedly conflicts with the meaning of the parable,[32] but what is meant by this is that it conflicts with a particular hypothetical reconstruction of the basic meaning of the parable! The strongest arguments in favor of the nonauthenticity of the interpretation of the parable involve the vocabulary found in these verses. The expression "close of the age" (v. 49) is found nowhere else in the New Testament except Matt 13:39, 40; 24:3; 28:20.[33] The expression "furnace of fire" (v. 50) is also restricted to Matthew in that the only other location of this expression is Matt 13:42. As for the latter part of v. 50, it is evident that this a Matthean expression because of its appearance in Matt 8:12; 13:42; 22:13; 24:51; 25:30. In the light of all this it would appear that the interpretation of our parable is either an expansion of Jesus' original interpretation or an authoritative interpretation which the Evangelist has given the parable.

What then was the meaning of the parable for Jesus? Like the parable of the wheat and the tares, this one deals with the final judgment. There is a day coming in which grace gives way to judgment. In that day a final and complete separation of the righteous and the unrighteous will take place. Now, however, there is still time. Therefore one should repent. Whether this parable was also told the disciples in order to impress upon them the need to be patient in that the kingdom of God has only come in part and that they must wait for God to bring about the final judgment in his own good time[34] is impossible to prove. What is clear is that Jesus warned of a final judgment, and that he urged his listeners to prepare themselves for it.

The Wheat and the Tares (Matt 13:24-30, 36-43)

This is another parable that deals with the final judgment:

> The kingdom of heaven may be compared to a man who sowed good seed in his field; but while men were sleeping, his enemy came and sowed weeds among the wheat and went away. So when the plants came up and bore grain, then the weeds appeared also. And the servants of the householder came and said to him, "Sir, did you not sow good seed in your field? How then has it weeds?" He said to them, "An enemy has done this." The servants said to him, "Then do you want us to go and gather them?" But he said, "No; lest in gathering the weeds you root up the wheat along with them. Let both grow together until the harvest; and at harvest time I will tell the reapers, Gather the weeds first and bind them in bundles to be burned, but gather the wheat into my barn." (Matt 13:24-30)

Added to this parable we find the following interpretation:

> Then he left the crowds and went into the house. And his disciples came to him, saying, "Explain to us the parable of the weeds of the

field." He answered, "He who sows the good seed is the Son of man; the field is the world, and the good seed means the sons of the kingdom; the weeds are the sons of the evil one, and the enemy who sowed them is the devil; the harvest is the close of the age, and the reapers are angels. Just as the weeds are gathered and burned with fire, so will it be at the close of the age. The Son of man will send his angels, and they will gather out of his kingdom all causes of sin and all evildoers, and throw them into the furnace of fire; there men will weep and gnash their teeth. Then the righteous will shine like the sun in the kingdom of their Father. He who has ears, let him hear." (Matt 13:36-43)

The authenticity of this parable and especially its interpretation have been greatly debated. The great majority of scholars argue for the view that the interpretation is essentially a Matthean creation, and for many Jeremias' analysis of this passage makes it "impossible to avoid the conclusion that the interpretation of the parable of the Tares is the work of Matthew himself."[35] Others have attempted to find in the interpretation a pre-Matthean layer of the tradition,[36] but in essence the interpretation is still seen as being primarily the work of Matthew. As for the parable, its authenticity is also greatly debated. Some see vs. 24b-26 as the authentic core;[37] others argue that the main core consists of 24b, 26b, 30b;[38] whereas others argue for the essential authenticity of the entire parable.[39] Since the parable does appear in the Gospel of Thomas 57 in a form closely resembling the form of the parable in Matthew[40] and since there are no essential internal tensions or contradictions in the parable, it seems best to treat the parable as basically authentic and recognize the Matthean terminology found in the parable as being an editorial rewording of Jesus' teaching in the terminology of the Evangelist rather than an extensive reworking of the parable by Matthew.[41]

What then is the point of the parable in the *Sitz im Leben* of Jesus? The scene portrayed in the parable is not a difficult one to picture. The kingdom of God is likened to the following scene: a man (householder) sowed seed on his field (no doubt by means of his servants) and shortly thereafter his enemy sowed seeds (tares/darnel = *Lolium tremulentum*) in the same field. When both sprouted and the weeds began to grow in greater than normal numbers, the servants reported this to their master. Because of the great similarity in the appearance of the wheat and the weeds, the householder told his servants to wait until harvesttime for their separation, lest in a premature attempt to separate the wheat and the weeds some of the wheat also be uprooted and destroyed. At the time of harvest, however, this separation is to be made, for at that time the wheat and the weeds which in their beginning stages appear remarkably alike are quite different, so that separation is much easier. Then the precious wheat is stored in the householder's granary and the weeds are tied into bundles for burning (no doubt to provide fuel for heat or cooking, MATT 6:30).

The parable clearly portrays a judgment scene in which a final separation is made. The parable is therefore closely related in theme to the parable of the great dragnet.[42] Yet by the addition of the "reapers" in v. 30 an added dimension is added to the parable. There is no basic need to deny the substantial authenticity of this image, for the Gospel of Thomas also makes a distinction between the "servants" and the "reapers" even though these specific terms are not used.

> The man did not allow them to pull up the weed. He said to them,
> Lest you go to pull up (*lit.*, that we may pull up) the weed, and you
> pull up the wheat along with it. For on the day of the harvest the
> weeds will appear; they will be pulled up and burned.[43]

It should be noted in the above translation that there is present the implication that servants (you) are not involved in the harvesting of the weeds. The passive construction "they will be pulled up and burned" implies that others will do the harvesting. There is good ground, therefore, for maintaining that the distinction between the "sowers" and the "reapers" in the parable is both authentic and of real significance. Jeremias has argued that this parable, like the parable of the great net, was meant by Jesus to impress upon his listeners the need for patience in that the final hour of judgment had not come.[44] The need for such teaching in the *Sitz im Leben* of Jesus was clearly manifest for several reasons. For one, the zealots and others were impatient and desired the separation of the wheat from the tares immediately and this meant for them the destruction of the Roman Empire. The Pharisees also may have criticized Jesus for his teaching that the kingdom of God had come in his ministry when there was with it no judgment of the wicked.[45] Qumran in its own way sought such a separation by isolating itself from the unrighteous and seeking to establish in the wilderness a community prepared for the coming of the Messiah by eliminating from its presence any "weeds." Even the disciples may have had similar needs, as John's and James's desire to bring fire down from heaven to consume the Samaritan "weeds" indicates (see Luke 9:51-56). Judgment, Jesus taught, was coming. There would be a final separation, but their task did not involve this separation. The "reapers" would come, and they would separate the wheat from the weeds. That this was the interpretation Jesus intended is evident by the fact that the harvesting, which was usually done by the servants, was to be performed by the reapers.[46]

If, for the sake of argument, we assume that the interpretation of the parable is essentially that of Matthew,[47] what can we learn concerning his interpretation of the parable?[48] Probably the key issue here involves the question of whether the "field" which is harvested represents for Matthew the "world" or the "kingdom," i.e., the church. If it is the former, then the scene involves the final judgment of the nations. If it is the latter, then the Evangelist has applied the parable to the idea that the church, too, will be judged and its present impure character rectified. For the present writer the latter possibility, if true, would mean that the Evangelist as an inspired interpreter of the words of Jesus has applied this parable to the situation of the "visible church" of his day and given an authoritative interpretation of the parable in this area of his concern.

The problem of knowing exactly what Matthew meant is due to the fact that in v. 38 the "field" is defined as the "world," and if one argues that "out of his kingdom" in v. 41 refers to the church, we have an apparent contradiction. There are at least three possible explanations of this that commend themselves. One is that the reference to the "field" as the "world" was present in the pre-Matthean source that the Evangelist used and that he misinterpreted this as a reference to the church. Another is that Matthew is responsible for the entire interpretation and was simply inconsistent between v. 38 and v. 41. In both these explanations we can posit either that Matthew was ignorant of this inconsistency or that he knew of it but did not care to resolve this inconsistency. A third possibility that commends itself more strongly still is the attempt, if possible, to see if vs. 36 and 41 can be "harmonized."[49] This may not be possible, but the attempt, at least, should be made to do so. What actually will take place when the Son of man returns in his glory? Is there not a sense in which when the Son of man returns "the kingdom of the world . . . [will] become the kingdom of our Lord and of his Christ" (Rev 11:15)? At his coming the Son of man is given dominion (Dan 7:14), so that the "world" becomes freed from the power of the Evil One and becomes the kingdom of the Son of man. At this time he will then "gather out of his kingdom" the unrighteous. This expression probably means no more than that the unrighteous shall not be permitted to enter the kingdom. This understanding of the expression is supported by MATT 8:11-12 where it is said that people will come from east and west to sit with the patriarchs in the kingdom of heaven but that the "sons of the kingdom will be thrown into the outer darkness."

> The Greek word, "will be cast out," indicates that the Jews who by history and covenant were "sons of the Kingdom" will be excluded from entering the Kingdom, not rejected after having once entered. So that statement that the evil are to be gathered "out of his kingdom" means no more than that they will be prevented from entering it.[50]

It should furthermore be pointed out that the view that the expression "kingdom" in v. 41 refers to the church is also not without its difficulties, in that there are no sayings of Jesus in Matthew where this association is clearly made.[51] It appears therefore far from certain that Matthew made or could have made such a one-to-one correspondence between the kingdom of heaven and the church.

It would seem best, then, not to equate the "kingdom" of v. 41 with the church. Rather we should see in this expression the consummation of the kingdom of heaven which will take place at the coming of the Son of man. "To gather out of his kingdom" would then mean to exclude from the new age, which now comes in its fullness and perfection, those who are unrighteous. When this kingdom comes (cf. MATT 6:10) through the parousia of the Son of man, the righteous who do the will of the Son shall enter (Matt 7:21) but many that day shall be "gathered out of the kingdom," i.e., will be excluded (MATT 7:22-23). Like John the Baptist foretold, the Son of man will come with "his winnowing fork . . . in his hand, and he will . . . gather his wheat into the granary, but the chaff he will burn with unquenchable fire" (MATT 3:12).[52] The goodness and grace of God should not be misunderstood. One should not "presume upon the riches of his kindness and forbearance and patience" (Rom 2:4). These are intended to lead us to repentance! The day is coming when the unrighteous will forever remain in their unrighteousness and the righteous will be confirmed in their righteousness.

CONCLUSION

In the last four chapters we have attempted to apply to the parables of Jesus the various principles of interpretation arrived at in Chapters 1-5. (Chapter 6 served as an example for this methodology.) Contained within the parables of Jesus are a number of various themes and emphases. We have investigated four of them. In Chapter 7 we noted that the parables contain in them the good news that in the ministry of Jesus the kingdom of God had indeed come. The long-awaited day had come, the promises of the Old Testament were being fulfilled; God was visiting his people. The messianic banquet was spread before them and all were invited to eat. In Chapter 8 we noted that with this joyous proclamation there also came a call to decision. Each hearer was called upon to respond, for "now is the acceptable time" (2 Cor 6:2). To hesitate was foolish, for nothing was to be gained whereas all could be lost. Yet why should one hesitate when one realizes what the God of the parables is like? In Chapter 9 we discovered how gracious, loving, and kind the God of the parables really is. To prodigals and sinners he freely offers forgiveness. Outcasts he bids enter. Only those boastful of their own piety and pride stumble over this God! Yet in Chapter 10 we also learned that a day is coming in which opportunity gives way to judgment and patience to punishment. The God of the parables is not only gracious and kind, but he is also holy and just! A day is coming which the very character of God demands. In that day there will be a final separation in which the sheep will be separated from the goats, the wheat from the chaff. Indeed this will be a terrible day and there will be "weeping and gnashing of teeth." Yet now the invitation to the great banquet is still open. So "come; for all is now ready" (Luke 14:17).

NOTES

CHAPTER 1.
WHAT IS A PARABLE?

1. For a fuller discussion of the languages of Jesus, see Robert H. Stein, *The Method and Message of Jesus' Teachings* (Westminster Press, 1978), pp. 4-6.

2. 1 Sam 24:14 in the Hebrew text and in the LXX.

3. The term "ballad singers" is used to translate *mashalim* in Num 21:27, but note that what they sing is a Taunt or Word of Derision.

4. In Deut 28:37; 1 Kings 9:7; and 2 Chron 7:20 the term "proverb" is used to translate *mashal*, but it is clearly a synonym for "horror" and "byword" in the former passage and "byword" in the latter two passages.

5. Ps 44:15 in the Hebrew text and 43:15 in the LXX.

6. Ps 69:12 in the Hebrew text and 68:12 in the LXX.

7. Ps 77:2 in the LXX.

8. Ps 49:5 in the Hebrew text and 48:5 in the LXX.

9. The term "proverbs" is again used to translate *mashal* in Prov 1:6, but note that it is a synonym for "riddle."

10. Ezek 21:5-10 in the Hebrew text and in the LXX.

11. For a more existential definition of these two terms, see Robert W. Funk, *Language, Hermeneutic, and Word of God* (Harper & Row, 1966), p. 137. Here Funk distinguishes between a simile and a metaphor by claiming that a simile is simply illustrative whereas a metaphor is creative of meaning, i.e., a means by which meaning is discovered.

12. See Eta Linnemann, *Parables of Jesus,* trans. by John Sturdy (London: SPCK, 1966), pp. 24-30, for an explanation of this terminology.

13. A more recent approach which has been used to distinguish between a parable and an allegory is given by John Dominic Crossan, *In Parables* (Harper & Row, 1973), pp. 8-15. Crossan defines an allegory as a metaphor in which "information precedes participation" whose aim is to illustrate. On the other hand, a parable is a metaphor in which "participation precedes information" whose aim is to bring about "participation in the metaphor's referent" (p. 14). Such a definition, however, seems to lose sight of the fact that an allegory can aim to bring about participation and a parable can aim to bring about

understanding! See below, pp. 65-70, for a discussion of this modern approach to the parables.

14. See below, pp. 54-55.

15. For a more "functional" categorization of the example parables, story parables, and "allegories" of Jesus, see Crossan, who uses the terms "parables of advent"; "parables of reversal"; and "parables of action."

16. Joachim Jeremias, *The Parables of Jesus*, trans. by S. H. Hooke, rev. ed. (Charles Scribner's Sons, 1963), p. 20, states that any attempt at defining exactly what a parable is becomes "a fruitless labour in the end," since the Hebrew *mashal* and the Aramaic equivalent *mathla* embrace all sorts of categories without distinction. Cf. also C. H. Dodd, *The Parables of the Kingdom* (London: James Nisbet & Co. 1935), p. 18.

17. A. R. Johnson, in *Wisdom in Israel and in the Ancient Near East*, ed. by M. Noth and D. Winton Thomas (Leiden: E. J. Brill, 1955), p. 162, in speaking of the etymology of the term *mashal* states, "There is no reason to doubt that basically the term implies 'likeness,' and the recognition of this fact is of first importance for understanding the different shades of meaning which it seems to have acquired."

18. There is a sense in which the term "parable" can become so broad that all of Jesus' teachings can be subsumed under it, for in MARK 4:11 it is said that Jesus taught "everything *[ta panta]* in parables" to those outside and to the disciples in MARK 4:34 "he did not speak . . . without a parable." See G. H. Boobyer, "The Redaction of Mark IV. 1-34," NTS, Vol. 8 (1961), p. 63.

19. The following designations are used in the text: a verse number in italic type indicates that the term *parabolē* is found in that verse, and a verse number in boldface italic type indicates that the following saying or story is introduced by an explicit comparison such as "like," "compare," "as if." Because all the parallel accounts of each parable are listed, we have dispensed in this section with the use of MARK-Mark, MATT-Matt, and LUKE-Luke.

20. The Gospel of Thomas (GT) is one of some fifty-two different works discovered in 1945-46 at Nag Hammadi in Upper Egypt. These works are contained in twelve books and are translations of earlier Greek works into the Coptic language. The Gospel of Thomas consists of a collection of 114 sayings of Jesus written probably in the middle of the second century. It is written from a Jewish Christian and especially a gnostic point of view. For a good summary of the contents of this work, see "Thomas, Gospel of" in *The Interpreter's Dictionary of the Bible* (Abingdon Press, 1976), Supp. Vol., pp. 902-905.

21. The sheep and the goats is included here as a "clear" parable even though the only pure parabolic element in this passage is the similitude of the shepherd separating the sheep and the goats in Matt 25:32-33.

CHAPTER 2.
WHY THE PARABLES?

1. See above, p. 20.

2. Vincent Taylor, *The Gospel According to St. Mark* (London: Macmillan & Co., 1952), p. 257, states concerning MARK 4:10-12, "This interpretation of the purpose of parables is so intolerable that from the earliest times it has been

questioned." T. W. Manson, *The Teaching of Jesus* (Cambridge University Press, 1931), p. 76, likewise states: "As the text stands, it can only mean that the object, or at any rate the result, of parabolic teaching is to prevent insight, understanding, repentance, and forgiveness. On any interpretation of parables this is simply absurd." Frederick C. Grant, "The Gospel According to St. Mark," in *The Interpreter's Bible* (Abingdon Press, 1951), Vol. 7, p. 700, is even more outspoken and states, "Mark's theory [Mark 4:10-12] can only be described as perverse." Cf. also Adolf Jülicher, *Die Gleichnisreden Jesu* (Tübingen: J. C. B. Mohr, 1910), Vol. I, p. 117, who states, "A correct and completely preserved parable required no explanatory word, does not even tolerate any, for everything in it is clear"; and W. Manson, "The Purpose of the Parables: A Re-examination of St. Mark iv. 10-12," ET, Vol. 68 (1956-57), p. 133.

3. See C. H. Peisker, "Konsecutives *hina* in Markus 4:12," ZNW, Vol. 59 (1968), pp. 126-127.

4. Otto Kaiser, *ISAIAH 1-12, A Commentary*, trans. by R. W. Wilson (The Old Testament Library) (Westminster Press, 1972), p. 83, states concerning this passage, "At the very moment of his call, Isaiah is consecrated to the purpose of hardening the heart of the people, a purpose God intends to pursue in sending him."

5. Jeremias, *The Parables of Jesus*, pp. 15-17, points out that the Markan form of the Isa 6:9-10 quotation follows the Targums in three ways: (1) the use of the third person rather than the second person in Isa 6:9b; (2) the use of "forgive" rather than "heal" in Isa 6:10; and (3) the use of the "divine passive" in Isa 6:10 rather than the active.

6. So Jeremias, *The Parables of Jesus*, p. 17, and Manson, *The Teaching of Jesus*, pp. 78-80. See also Hermann L. Strack & Paul Billerbeck, *Kommentar zum Neuen Testament aus Talmud und Midrash* (Munich: C. H. Beck'sche Verlagsbuchhandlung, 1956), Vol. I, pp. 662-663, for four examples of the rabbinical exegesis of Isa 6:10b in which this passage is understood as being a promise of forgiveness rather than a threat for final hardening.

7. Manson, *The Teaching of Jesus*, pp. 78-80.

8. So Dodd, *The Parables of the Kingdom*, p. 3.

9. Whereas it is evident that these are indeed Markan themes, there is certainly no need to consider them as *de novo* Markan creations, for there is good reason to think that these themes stem back ultimately to Jesus, himself. Although somewhat dated, Vincent Taylor, "The Messianic Secret in Mark," ET, Vol. 59 (1947-48), pp. 146-151, and "W. Wrede's *The Messianic Secret in the Gospels*," ET, Vol. 65 (1953-54), pp. 246-250, are still essential reading on the subject and demonstrate that this theme can be traced back to Jesus. Furthermore, whereas Mark in Mark 11:1 to 13:37 clearly in his redaction reveals a Markan emphasis on the judgment and rejection of Israel, it is also clear that this theme goes back to Jesus as well. Note such passages as MARK 12:1-12; 13:1-2; LUKE 13:34-35; Luke 19:41-44; 23:27-31; Matt 23:29-36; etc.

10. So Jeremias, *The Parables of Jesus*, p. 15; Manson, *The Teaching of Jesus*, p. 77.

11. C. F. D. Moule, *An Idiom Book of New Testament Greek* (Cambridge University Press, 1959), p. 142, states that "the Semitic mind was notoriously unwilling to draw a sharp dividing-line between purpose and consequence."

12. See Edmund F. Sutcliffe, "Effect as Purpose: A Study in Hebrew Thought Patterns," *Biblica*, Vol. 35 (1954), pp. 320-327. See Moule, *An Idiom*

Book of New Testament Greek, p. 143, who states that we should understand both the *hina* and the *mēpote* as instances of the Semitic blurring of purpose and result.

13. The traditional bifurcation of "Greek thinking" and "Hebrew thinking" was rightfully dealt a devastating blow by James Barr's *The Semantics of Biblical Language* (London: Oxford University Press, 1961). We now realize that even as the Semitic world was influenced by the Greek world from the time of Alexander the Great on, so the West was likewise influenced by the East. As a result there did not exist an absolute distinction between Greek and Semitic cultures. Palestinian Judaism, itself, was greatly influenced by Hellenism. Nevertheless there were differences. More important for us, however, is the question of whether Jesus and the disciples may have thought less from the perspective of "purpose to result" than we do today. A good example of this is the term "foreknow," or *proginōskein*. It is now evident that instead of interpreting this term along the lines of Western philosophical tradition as implying knowing something beforehand, it is better to understand it from the Old Testament's point of view as the setting of one's (usually God's) affection upon someone (usually Israel).

14. So Jeremias, *The Parables of Jesus*, p. 17; Willi Marxsen, "Redaktionsgeschichtliche Erklärung der sogenannten Parabeltheorie des Markus," ZTK, Vol. 52 (1955), p. 269.

15. A. M. Ambrozic, "Mark's Concept of the Parable," CBQ, Vol. 29 (1967), p. 221, also points out that Mark does not work with a promise-fulfillment scheme which such an interpretation requires.

16. Matthew Black, *An Aramaic Approach to the Gospels and Acts* (Oxford: At the Clarendon Press, 1946), p. 155, states that it is certain that Mark actually wrote and intended *hina . . . mēpote,* and that his original purpose is clear from the *hina* clause and is reinforced by the *mēpote.*

17. J. Arthur Baird, "A Pragmatic Approach to Parable Exegesis: Some New Evidence on Mark 4:11, 33-34," JBL, Vol. 76 (1957), pp. 201-207. See also Raymond E. Brown, *The Semitic Background of the Term "Mystery" in the New Testament* (Fortress Press, 1968), pp. 34-35.

18. The following quote of Brown, *The Semitic Background*, p. 35 n. 110, seems reasonable. "Thus, seemingly, Jesus did not explain the parables dealing with the kingdom to outsiders, unless we are to presume an exceedingly technical rearrangement of the whole parable tradition by the Synoptics."

19. If, for instance, the probability of *hina* meaning "in order that what the Scriptures say may be fulfilled" is 50 percent and of *mēpote* meaning "unless" is 50 percent, the chance of both meaning this is only 25 percent!

20. See J. R. Kirkland, "The Earliest Understanding of Jesus' Use of Parables: Mark IV 10-12 in Context," NT, Vol. 19 (1977), pp. 1-4, and David Daube, *The New Testament and Rabbinic Judaism* (London: Athlone Press, 1956). Daube points out that "from the beginning, the form in question [the parables] is anything but universalistic" (p. 149).

21. See in this regard the Psalms of Solomon 17:23-24!

22. It should be noted that whereas Matt 13:11 and Luke 8:10 use the plural myster*ies*, MARK 4:11 uses the singular myster*y*. In this, Mark is in close agreement with Paul, who uses the singular in Rom 11:25 and in all other places but 1 Cor 4:1; 13:2; and 14:2.

20. Even if Luke 15 is a Lukan collection of parables uttered at different times, and it probably is, the context is certainly correct, and Jesus' use of these parables was in part at least to disarm his audience.

CHAPTER 3.
WHENCE THE PARABLES?

1. Cf. Jeremias, *The Parables of Jesus*, p. 11, who states: "Everywhere behind the Greek text [of the parables] we get glimpses of Jesus' mother tongue. Also the pictorial element of the parables is drawn from the daily life of Palestine."

2. Jubilees 11:11.

3. b. Shab. 73b. Cf. also b. Shab. 7.2. See Jeremias, *The Parables of Jesus*, p. 11 n. 3, for bibliography. For the contrary view, see John Drury, "The Sower, the Vineyard, and the Place of Allegory in the Interpretation of the Parables," JTS, Vol. 24 (1973), pp. 367-370.

4. See Dodd, *The Parables of the Kingdom*, p. 97, and Jeremias, *The Parables of Jesus*, pp. 74-76. For the contrary view, see Drury, "The Sower," p. 373, but S. Applebaum, "Economic Life in Palestine," in *The Jewish People in the First Century*, ed. by S. Safrai and M. Stern (Fortress Press, 1974), Vol. II, p. 660, states: "In general, the increase of state domain from the later Hasmonaean epoch onward and the expropriation of Jewish settlers from the coastal region and Transjordan by Pompey must have greatly increased the tenant-class."

5. Apparently a law(s) did exist which permitted the tenants to claim the land which they farmed if the owner died without heirs. See Jeremias, *The Parables of Jesus*, p. 75; Charles E. Carlston, *The Parables of the Triple Tradition* (Fortress Press, 1975), p. 184; and especially J. Duncan M. Derrett, *Law in the New Testament* (London: Darton, Longman & Todd, 1970), pp. 300-306.

6. Josephus, *The Jewish War*, II. viii. 1; cf. also Acts 5:37.

7. The translation of the term "bad" as implying that the fish were rotten seems incorrect, since rotten fish cannot swim into a net. They must therefore have been bad in the sense that they were uneatable, i.e., ceremonially unclean (cf. Lev 11:9-12; Deut 14:9-10).

8. Note here James 5:4.

9. See A. W. Argyle, "Wedding Customs at the Time of Jesus," ET, Vol. 86 (1975), pp. 214-216, and Jeremias, *The Parables of Jesus*, pp. 172-173.

10. For a detailed discussion and evaluation of this criterion, see Robert H. Stein, "The Criteria for Authenticity," in *Gospel Perspectives: Studies of History and Tradition in the Four Gospels*, ed. by R. T. France and David Wenham (Sheffield, England: JSOT Press, 1980), Vol. I, pp. 240-245.

11. Cf. John Dominic Crossan, "The Seed Parables of Jesus," JBL, Vol. 92 (1973), p. 263, who states, "When dissimilarity is applied to the form of Jesus' teaching and not just to the content, the parables are vindicated as authentic because the primitive church does not use this form itself, is not at home with Jesus' usage, and extensively modifies that usage in different ways."

12. See Joachim Jeremias, *New Testament Theology*, trans. by John Bowden (Charles Scribner's Sons, 1971), p. 29.

13. See Stein, *The Method and Message of Jesus' Teachings*, pp. 60-111.

14. Cf. Archibald M. Hunter, *The Parables Then and Now* (Westminster Press, 1972), pp. 14-15; Jeremias, *New Testament Theology,* p. 30.

15. Josephus, *Antiquities,* 17.318.

16. So Linnemann, *Parables of Jesus,* p. 108.

CHAPTER 4.

HOW THE PARABLES WERE INTERPRETED

1. For a helpful discussion of the rise of allegorical interpretation in the early church, see R. P. C. Hanson, *Allegory and Event* (John Knox Press, 1959), pp. 97-129.

2. See Werner Monselewski, *Der barmherzige Samariter* (Tübingen: J. C. B. Mohr, 1967), pp. 18-21.

3. Irenaeus, *Against Heresies* IV. xxxvi. 7.

4. Ibid., IV. xxvi. 1.

5. Ibid., III. xvii. 3.

6. In his *On Purity* 9, Tertullian states: "We, however, do not take the parables as sources of doctrine, but rather we take doctrine as a norm for interpreting the parables. Therefore we make no effort to twist everything so that it fits our own explanation, striving to avoid every discrepancy. Why a 'hundred' sheep? and why, indeed, 'ten' drachmas? and what does that 'broom' stand for? Well, when he wanted to show how pleased God is at the salvation of one sinner, he had to mention *some* numerical quantity from which *one* could be described as 'lost.' And in view of the ordinary procedure of a woman who looks for a drachma in the house, he had to supply the assistance of a broom and lamp. Curious questions of this sort lead to conclusions which are suspect and, as a rule, they seduce men from truth through the subtleties of an artificial exegesis." This translation comes from Tertullian, *Treatises on Penance,* trans. by William P. Le Saint (Ancient Christian Writers, No. 28) (Newman Press, 1959), p. 75.

7. Tertullian, *On Modesty,* Ch. 9.

8. Clement, *Who Is the Rich Man That Shall Be Saved?* XXIX.

9. See Origen, *On First Principles* IV. ii. 8. For a discussion of the role of the literal interpretation of the text for Origen, see Hanson, *Allegory and Event,* pp. 237-238.

10. Origen, *On First Principles* IV. i. 11-12 and IV. ii. 4.

11. Origen, *Commentary on Luke* 10:30-35 (Homily XXXIV).

12. See Hanson, *Allegory and Event,* pp. 134-161.

13. Ambrose, *Concerning Repentance* I. vii. 28 and I. xi. 51-52.

14. Augustine, *Quaestiones Evangeliorum* 2. 19.

15. John Chrysostom, *Matt Hom* lxiv. 3 (NPNF). Cf., however, *Matt Hom* lxxviii., where Chrysostom interprets the parable of the wise and foolish virgins allegorically!

16. The fourfold sense of Scripture probably owes its origin to John Cassian (d. 435) who in his *Conlationes* XIV c. 8 (CSEL 13/2, 404) described the three spiritual, i.e., nonliteral, senses as the tropological, the allegorical, and the anagogical. Earlier Augustine had also listed four senses of Scriptures (historical, allegorical, analogical, and aetiological). See his *De Genesi ad Litteram Imperfectus Liber,* c. 2, n. 5 (PL 34, 222) and *De Utilitate Credendi,* c. 3 (PL

42, 68f.), but it was Cassian's classification which was adopted. See James Samuel Preus, *From Shadow to Promise* (Harvard University Press, 1969), pp. 21-22.

17. This example comes from Cassian, *Conlationes* XIV c. 8.

18. Venerable Bede, *Lucae Evangelium Expositio*, lib. III (PL 92, 467-470).

19. For additional examples of how the parable of the good Samaritan was interpreted during this period, as well as the earlier and subsequent periods of the church, see Monselewski, *Der barmherzige Samariter*.

20. See Thomas Aquinas, *Summa Theologica*, Part 1, Question 1, Article 10.

21. Thomas Aquinas, *Catena Aurea* on Luke 10:29-37.

22. See Frederic W. Farrar, *History of Interpretation* (London: Macmillan & Co., 1886), p. 328.

23. For additional criticism of Origen and the allegorical method by Luther, see *Luther's Works*, ed. by Jaroslav Pelikan (Concordia Publishing House, 1958): "senseless allegories after the manner of Origen" (Vol. I, p. 122); "such destructive and foolish absurdities" (Vol. I, p. 185); "nonsensical allegories" (Vol. I, p. 231); "empty speculations and the froth . . . of the Holy Scriptures" (Vol. I, p. 233); "But I have often declared that I greatly abhor allegories and condemn the fondness for them" (Vol. V, p. 345); "I hate allegories" (Vol. V, p. 347). Luther did not, however, deny outright the use of allegory, but demanded that "those who want to make use of allegories base them on the historical account itself" (Vol. I, p. 233; see also Vol. III, p. 27).

24. See Luther's *Sermon on Romans* 12:3 and especially his *Sermon on Luke* 10:23-37. The latter is not easy to find but is contained in *The Precious and Sacred Writings of Martin Luther*, ed. by John Nicholas Lenker (Minneapolis: Lutherans in All Lands Co., 1905), XIV, pp. 26f.

25. John Calvin, *A Harmony of the Gospels Matthew, Mark and Luke*, trans. by A. W. Morrison (Wm. B. Eerdmans Publishing Co., 1972), Vol. III, pp. 38-39.

26. Ibid., p. 38.

27. Ibid., Vol. II, pp. 111-112.

28. Ibid., Vol. II, p. 265.

29. This does not mean, of course, that Calvin was "without sin" in this area. In his interpretation of the parable of the evil tenants (MARK 12:1-12, ibid., Vol. III, pp. 16-19) he allegorizes the parable as follows:

the vineyard = the church
tenants = pastors/priests
winepress = sacrifice
tower = other rites

30. *Corpus Reformatorum*, Vol. 25, pp. 380ff.

31. R. C. Trench, *Notes on the Parables of Our Lord* (New York: Appleton, 1866), pp. 258-264.

CHAPTER 5.
HOW THE PARABLES ARE INTERPRETED

1. In his *Die Gleichnisreden Jesu* I, p. 69, Jülicher refers to Aristotle's *Rhetoric* 2, 20, 2ff. where a parable is defined as a comparison *(Gleichnis)*, and in I, p. 51, he refers to Cicero's *Orator* 27.94, where Cicero states, "When there is a

continuous stream of metaphors, a wholly different style of speech is produced; consequently, the Greeks call it *allegoria* or 'allegory' " (Loeb).

2. Christian A. Bugge, *Die Haupt-Parabeln Jesu* (Giessen: A. Töpelmann, 1903).

3. Paul Fiebig, *Altjüdische Gleichnisse und die Geschichte Jesu* (Tübingen: J. C. B. Mohr, 1904).

4. Ibid., p. 98. For the opposing view see, however, Rudolf Bultmann, *The History of the Synoptic Tradition*, trans. by John Marsh (Harper & Row, 1968), p. 198.

5. See pp. 16-18.

6. Some more recent writers who have acknowledged the presence of allegory in the parables of Jesus are Maxime Hermaniuk, *La Parabole Évangélique* (Louvain: Bibliotheca Alfonsiana, 1947); Matthew Black, "The Parables as Allegory," BJRL, Vol. 42 (1959-60), pp 273-287; Raymond E. Brown, "Parable and Allegory Reconsidered," NT, Vol. 5 (1962), pp. 36-45; C. F. D. Moule, "Mark 4:1-20 Yet Once More," in *Neotestamentica et Semitica: Studies in Honour of Matthew Black*, ed. by E. Earle Ellis and Max Wilcox (Edinburgh: T. & T. Clark, 1969), pp. 95-113; Madeleine Boucher, *The Mysterious Parable: A Literary Study* (Catholic Biblical Association of America, 1977), pp. 11-25.

7. "Allegorically" is defined here as the finding of two levels of meaning in an allusion, detail, or the parable itself, outside of the basic point of comparison in the parable. To the extent that a parable serves as a comparison (something is likened to something else), there must be present a basic two-level comparison. In the parable of the prodigal son/loving father we find the following comparison: younger son = publicans and sinners; older son = scribes and Pharisees; father = God or Jesus. Acknowledging this comparison is not "allegorizing." "Allegorizing" means to go beyond the one basic metaphorical comparison and see two levels of meaning in such terms as: ring = Christian baptism; feast = Lord's Supper; fatted calf = sacrifice of Christ; robe = divine sonship; etc. At times such terms may serve as "tropes" and have two levels of meaning, but if the history of interpretation reveals anything, it is that there is present more of a tendency to see additional meaning in the details of the parables when they are not actually present than to ignore such additional levels of meaning when they are present. The determining factor for concluding if such a trope possesses two levels of meaning is the intention of the author (Jesus/the Evangelist).

8. Two additional examples of Jülicher which can be cited involve the parables of the laborers in the vineyard (Matt 20:1-16) and the good Samaritan (Luke 10:29-36). In the former the one point is that "there is one salvation for all mankind" (*Die Gleichnisreden Jesu*, II, 467); in the latter the one point is that "the most important duty for man is to love!" (II, 596).

9. In seeking to ascertain if Jesus intended any allegorical significance by the details in the parable, we often find it helpful to see if there are present any details or items which had symbolic significance for Jesus' first-century Jewish audience.

10. See below, pp. 98-106, for a more detailed discussion of the parable of the hidden treasure and of the pearl.

11. Calvin, *A Harmony of the Gospels Matthew, Mark and Luke*, Vol. II, p. 112.

12. See below, pp. 106 111, for a more detailed discussion of this parable.

13. For a recent attempt to defend the multiplicity of meanings which the early church found in the parables, see: David C. Steinmetz, "The Superiority of Pre-Critical Exegesis," *Theology Today*, Vol. 37 (1980), pp. 27-38.

14. W. H. Robinson, *The Parables of Jesus in Their Relation to His Ministry* (University of Chicago Press, 1928).

15. A. T. Cadoux, *The Parables of Jesus: Their Art and Use* (London: J. Clarke, 1930).

16. C. H. Dodd, *The Parables of the Kingdom* (Charles Scribner's Sons, 1936), p. 32.

17. Ibid., p. 174.

18. For a discussion of Jesus' teachings on the kingdom of God, see Stein, *The Method and Message of Jesus' Teachings*, pp. 65-79.

19. Jeremias, *The Parables of Jesus*, Foreword.

20. Note, for instance, Joachim Jeremias, *Jerusalem in the Time of Jesus*, trans. by F. H. and C. H. Cave (Fortress Press, 1969).

21. In the light of Jeremias' view that "the gospel of Jesus and the kerygma of the early church must not be placed on the same footing, but they are related to one another as call and response" (*The Problem of the Historical Jesus*, trans. by Norman Perrin, p. 23; Fortress Press, 1964), it is not surprising to see under his name such titles as *The Parables of Jesus; The Eucharistic Words of Jesus; The Lord's Prayer; The Prayers of Jesus; New Testament Theology: The Proclamation of Jesus; The Sermon on the Mount; The Unknown Sayings of Jesus;* etc.

22. Hans Conzelmann, *Die Mitte der Zeit* (Tübingen: J. C. B. Mohr, 1954). The English translation is *The Theology of St. Luke*, trans. by Geoffrey Buswell (Harper & Brothers, 1960).

23. Willi Marxsen, *Der Evangelist Markus: Studien zur Redaktionsgeschichte des Evangeliums* (Göttingen: Vandenhoeck & Ruprecht, 1959). The English translation is *Mark the Evangelist: Studies on the Redaction History of the Gospel*, trans. by James Boyce, Donald Juel, William R. Poehlmann with Roy A. Harrisville (Abingdon Press, 1969).

24. For a discussion of the rise and aims of redaction criticism, see Robert H. Stein, "What Is Redaktionsgeschichte?" *JBL*, Vol. 88 (1969), pp. 45-56.

25. Two recent works that deal with the parables from a structuralist point of view are *Semiology and Parables*, ed. by Daniel Patte (Pittsburgh Theological Monograph Series, Vol. 9) (Pickwick Press, 1976), and *Signs and Parables*, ed. by Dikran Y. Hadidan (Pittsburgh Theological Monograph Series, Vol. 23) (Pickwick Press, 1978).

26. Some important works in this area are Geraint Vaughan Jones, *The Art and Truth of the Parables* (London: SPCK, 1964); Amos Wilder, *The Language of the Gospel: Early Christian Rhetoric* (Harper & Row, 1964); Robert W. Funk, *Language, Hermeneutic, and Word of God: The Problem of Language in the New Testament and Contemporary Language* (Harper & Row, 1966); Dan Otto Via, Jr., *The Parables: Their Literary and Existential Dimension* (Fortress Press, 1967); John Dominic Crossan, *In Parables: The Challenge of the Historical Jesus* (Harper & Row, 1973), and *Cliffs of Fall: Paradox and Polyvalence in the Parables of Jesus* (Seabury Press, 1980); Sallie McFague TeSelle, *Speaking in Parables* (Fortress Press, 1975); Madeleine Boucher, *The Mysterious Parable* (Catholic Biblical Association of America, 1977); Mary Ann Tolbert, *Perspectives on the Parables: An Approach to*

Multiple Interpretations (Fortress Press, 1979); one should also note the *Semeia* series (Vols. 1, 2, 9) published by Scholar's Press in Missoula.

27. Susan Wittig, "A Theory of Multiple Meanings," *Semeia*, Vol. 9 (1977), p. 82.

28. Cf. Leonard L. Thompson, *Introducing Biblical Language* (Prentice-Hall, 1978), p. 5, who speaks of the "world-creating power of language."

29. Funk, *Language, Hermeneutic, and Word of God*, p. 137. Cf. also Crossan, *In Parables*, p. 14, who states that parables are "metaphors in which participation precedes information so that the function of metaphor is to create participation in the metaphor's referent."

30. See Crossan, *Cliffs of Fall*, p. 8, who speaks of the "ubiquitous" quality of metaphor!

31. So Via, *The Parables*, pp. 77-88. For a negative critique of this view, see Boucher, *The Mysterious Parable*, pp. 14-17.

32. See TeSelle, *Speaking in Parables*, pp. 71-72.

33. Eberhard Jüngel, *Paulus und Jesus* (Tübingen: J. C. B. Mohr, 1962), p. 135. The present writer makes no claim of understanding what Jüngel means by this.

34. Boucher, *The Mysterious Parable*, p. 27, rightly points out: "Surely the first circle of hearers, those who heard the parables from the lips of Jesus, asked, 'What does the man mean?' They must have wondered, that is about his intention."

35. It should be noted that "many such parables" is in the instrumental case in Greek!

36. It is clear that in the third *Sitz im Leben* the Evangelists understood the parables, at least in part, to be teaching *about* the kingdom of God. A good example of this is Luke's use of the parable of the pounds (Luke 19:11-27). Whatever its function may have been in the first *Sitz im Leben*, in Luke it serves the purpose of teaching his reader(s) about the delay of the parousia (see above, pp. 64-65). It is also evident that the parable of the evil tenants (MARK 12:1-11) does not have in Mark an existential function of self-understanding but rather a didactic function of teaching about God's judgment upon Israel. If a parable can serve in the third *Sitz im Leben* a strongly didactic function, can anyone then claim *a priori* that a parable could not serve such a function in the first *Sitz im Leben* or our own *Sitz im Leben*?

37. For the opposing view, see Crossan, *In Parables*, p. 10.

38. Raymond E. Brown, "Hermeneutics," in *The Jerome Biblical Commentary*, ed. by Raymond E. Brown, Joseph A. Fitzmyer, Roland E. Murphy (Prentice-Hall, 1969), p. 607.

39. Hyam Maccoby, "Gospel and Midrash," *Commentary*, Vol. 69 (1980), p. 72, states: "The study of the Gospels as pure literature is certainly an interesting and worthwhile activity. But it should not be forgotten that the Gospels were not written as pure literature. Any work that has an extra-literary aim in view, such as the propagation of a political or religious standpoint, cannot be assessed without asking what the author is trying to prove and what we as readers and moral beings think of the attitude that the author is so passionately trying to persuade us to adopt."

40. Boucher, *The Mysterious Parable*, p. 32, is correct therefore when she states, "Only an interpretation which stays within the limits of the original intention of Jesus is a valid one!"

CHAPTER 6.

INTERPRETING THE PARABLES TODAY

1. Jeremias, *The Parables of Jesus*, p. 202.
2. T. W. Manson, *The Sayings of Jesus* (London: SCM Press, 1949), p. 260.
3. Jeremias, *The Parables of Jesus*, p. 205.
4. MATT 18:21-22; LUKE 6:27-28; MATT 5:38-42; etc.
5. The form of Luke 10:25-37 resembles in many ways Luke 7:36-50. Both parables are connected with an incident. The former involves Jesus' teaching of the love command; the latter, the anointing of Jesus. In both instances the parable is concluded with a question in which Jesus' opponent is forced to complete the parable (Luke 10:36 and 7:43), and in both instances there is a similar misconception. In the former it involves what it means to be a "neighbor"; in the latter it involves what it means to be a "prophet."
6. So Linnemann, *Parables of Jesus*, p. 138.
7. See Josephus, *Antiquities*, 18.2.2 or 18.30.
8. Linnemann, *Parables of Jesus*, p. 54.
9. Jones, *The Art and Truth of the Parables*, p. 258.
10. Jeremias, *The Parables of Jesus*, p. 204.
11. Ibid., p. 205.
12. Clarence Jordan, *The Cotton Patch Version of Luke and Acts* (Association Press, 1969), pp. 46-47.

CHAPTER 7.

THE KINGDOM OF GOD AS A PRESENT REALITY

1. See below, n. 6.
2. See Linnemann, *Parables of Jesus*, pp. 166-167.
3. See "Meals," *The Oxford Classical Dictionary*, 2d ed., ed. by N. G. L. Hammond and H. H. Scullard (Oxford: At the Clarendon Press, 1970), p. 658.
4. See Strack-Billerbeck, *Kommentar zum Neuen Testament aus Talmud und Midrash*, Vol. II, pp. 202, 204-206.
5. Note Ex 16:12; Judg 19:16-21; and especially Matt 20:6, 12, where the last workers, hired the eleventh hour (5 P.M.), worked one hour. The evening meal would therefore have to follow after work was over, i.e., after 6 P.M.
6. Although it is not as clear as in Luke, Matthew and the Gospel of Thomas also portray a two-stage invitation. In Matt 22:2-3, we read "The kingdom of heaven may be compared to a king who gave a marriage feast for his son, and sent his servants to call *those who were invited* to the marriage feast" (italics added). The perfect participle (*keklēmenous*) indicates that they had received (and accepted the first invitation) and now were receiving the second invitation telling them that the feast was ready. In the Gospel of Thomas 64, we read, "Jesus said: A man *had guests*, and when he had prepared the banquet . . ., he sent his servant to summon the guests," italics added (*Synopsis Quattuor Evangeliorum*; Stuttgart: Deutsche Bibelstiftung, 1978). The fact that the man had guests indicates that here, too, a prior invitation, which had been accepted, is envisioned.
7. Jeremias, *The Parables of Jesus*, p. 176.

8. So Linnemann, *Parables of Jesus*, p. 89.

9. Jeremias, *The Parables of Jesus*, pp. 178-179.

10. So I. Howard Marshall, *The Gospel of Luke* (New International Greek Testament Commentary) (Wm. B. Eerdmans Publishing Co., 1978), p. 587.

11. So Linnemann, *Parables of Jesus*, p. 163 n. 10.

12. Both Matthew (22:2) and Luke (14:16) emphasize that this was a great banquet ("marriage feast," Matthew). The Gospel of Thomas describes it simply as a banquet. In Rev 19:9 the bliss of the kingdom is also described in terms of a banquet: "Blessed are those who are invited to the marriage supper of the Lamb."

13. Linnemann, *Parables of Jesus*, pp. 88-89, 159-162.

14. Jeremias, *The Parables of Jesus*, p. 178, n. 3.

15. Even if it were granted for the sake of argument that the purpose of the parable was primarily apologetical, this would not eliminate the eschatological element in the parable, for the apologetic would center around Jesus' behavior in inviting the outcasts to the (eschatological) banquet!

16. So Derrett, *Law in the New Testament*, pp. 126-155. Cf. also Paul H. Ballard, "Reasons for Refusing the Great Supper," JTS, Vol. 23 (1977), pp. 341-350. For a helpful criticism of Derrett's thesis, see Humphrey Palmer, "Just Married, Cannot Come," NT, Vol. 18 (1976), pp. 241-257.

17. Derrett, *Law in the New Testament*, p. 141.

18. In favor of the greater authenticity of the Lukan account we should take note of the following: (1) the Gospel of Thomas stands in *much closer* agreement with the Lukan account than with the Matthean account, so that it is probable that the earlier form of the parable resembled the Lukan and the Gospel of Thomas version rather than the Matthean version and (2) the presence of various allegorical details in Matthew (the testament of the servants which seems strange; the destruction of Jerusalem) appear secondary.

19. For a discussion of the realized dimension of Jesus' teaching about the kingdom of God, see Stein, *The Method and Message of Jesus' Teachings*, pp. 68-72, 75-79.

20. Linnemann, *Parables of Jesus*, p. 92.

21. Jeremias, *The Parables of Jesus*, p. 177, points out that "even the poorest, with oriental courtesy, modestly resist the invitation to the entertainment until they are taken by the hand and gently forced to enter the house."

22. See above, pp. 78-79.

23. See MARK 11:17; 12:9; LUKE 13:29; cf. John 4:20-23.

24. See b. Taan 10a.

25. TDNT, Vol. I, pp. 76-77.

26. See LUKE 14:15-24; MATT 22:1-10. Cf. also MARK 14:25.

27. In the Old Testament and the Jewish literature of Jesus' day the image of the bridegroom does not appear to have been used as a messianic designation. Even if such a reference were to be found, it is clear that the expression was not a common messianic designation. It would seem, therefore, that the messianic claim of Jesus found in this parable should be understood as being in keeping with the veiled claims that preceded the events of Caesarea Philippi.

28. It should be noted that the verbal tenses in MARK 4:30-32 and MATT 13:33 are all aorists. The present form of these parables at least places no emphasis on any process of growth.

29. TDNT, Vol. III, p. 811, n. 1

30. See Jeremias, *The Parables of Jesus*, p. 148.

31. Frequently the reference to the birds resting and making their nests in the branches of the mustard "tree" is seen as an allegorical reference to the entrance of the Gentiles into the kingdom of God. (So Jeremias, *The Parables of Jesus*, p. 147.) The birds, however, are not a separate metaphor but rather a means of emphasizing the size of the final product.

32. Two aspects of the parable of the leaven have frequently troubled interpreters. These involve the large amount of flour (three *sata* or approximately fifty pounds of flour) and the term *enekrupsen* or "hidden" where we would expect something like "placed," "put," "mixed," etc. Attempts to see behind the large amount of flour needed for baking for a large banquet are unnecessary. The large amount of flour serves simply to indicate the largeness of the final product—fifty pounds of raised flour. The use of the term "hidden" does seem intentional, however, and may allude to the "hiddenness" of the kingdom of God in its present manifestation.

33. The two parallels to this parable found in MATT 16:3-4 and GT 91 refer to different "signs," but it is clear that they also refer to the signs of the new age. In the former we have a reference to the "signs of the times" and in the latter to "this time."

34. Cf. Assumption of Moses 10:1.

35. Cf. also the eschatological signs Jesus calls to the attention of John the Baptist in MATT 11:4-6.

CHAPTER 8.
THE KINGDOM OF GOD AS DEMAND—THE CALL TO DECISION

1. Jeremias, *The Parables of Jesus*, p. 230.

2. Both translations are those of Bruce M. Metzger in *Synopsis Quattuor Evangeliorum* (Stuttgart: Deutsche Bibelstiftung, 1978).

3. So James M. Robinson (ed.), *The Nag Hammadi Library* (Harper & Row, 1977), p. 117; John H. Sieber, "A Redactional Analysis of the Synoptic Gospels with Regard to the Question of the Sources of the Gospel According to Thomas" (unpublished Ph.D. dissertation, Claremont Graduate School, 1965), especially pp. 260-263.

4. See, however, John C. Fenton, "The Parables of the Treasure and the Pearl (Mt 13:44-46)," ET, Vol. 77 (1966), p. 180, and Jeremias, *The Parables of Jesus*, p. 199, for the view that the Gospel of Thomas may be more original with regard to certain aspects such as the description of the merchant as a pearl merchant.

5. Jeremias, *The Parables of Jesus*, p. 90.

6. Rudolf Bultmann, *The History of the Synoptic Tradition*, trans. by John Marsh (Harper & Row, 1963), p. 173.

7. Derrett, "Law in the New Testament: The Treasure in the Field (Mt. XIII, 44)," ZNW, Vol. 54 (1963), pp. 31-42.

8. Ibid., p. 35.

9. See Linnemann, *Parables of Jesus*, p. 98.

10. So Jeremias, *The Parables of Jesus*, p. 199; Derrett, "Law in the New Testament," p. 35.

11. Cf. Linnemann, *Parables of Jesus*, pp. 98-99, who states: "If it is not morally a hundred per cent unobjectionable, this is unimportant as is the question whether the finder's 'action was formally legitimate' or not. It is part of the stage-management of the narrator that the finder does not remove the treasure, but buries it again, so as to acquire it together with the field. Only so can the point of comparison which the narrator has in mind be brought out from this material." Cf. also Jack Dean Kingsbury, *The Parables of Jesus in Matthew 13* (John Knox Press, 1969), p. 112.

12. Jeremias, *The Parables of Jesus* p. 199. See also n. 3, above.

13. Even though the Gospel of Thomas describes the person who bought the pearl simply as a "merchant," this merchant must have been familiar enough with pearls to recognize the great value of what he had found. As a result it may be premature to claim that the description of the person as a pearl merchant in Matthew is secondary.

14. So Linnemann, *Parables of Jesus*, p. 99.

15. See Otto Glombitza, "Der Perlenkaufmann," NTS, Vol. 7 (1960), p. 157.

16. Cf. Linnemann, *Parables of Jesus*, pp. 16-17.

17. See Kingsbury, *The Parables of Jesus in Matthew 13*, pp. 113-114.

18. So Dodd, *The Parables of the Kingdom*, p. 86, and Linnemann, *Parables of Jesus*, p. 99, note g.

19. So Kingsbury, *The Parables of Jesus in Matthew 13*, p. 116.

20. Linnemann, *Parables of Jesus*, p. 100.

21. Dodd, *The Parables of the Kingdom*, p. 87.

22. See Stein, *The Method and Message of Jesus' Teachings*, p. 96.

23. So Kingsbury, *The Parables of Jesus in Matthew 13*, p. 116.

24. Ibid., p. 115.

25. It should be noted that the same Greek word is used for "master" in Luke 16:8 and "Lord" in 18:6.

26. See I. H. Marshall, "Luke XVI, 8—Who Commended the Unjust Steward?" JTS, Vol. 19 (1968), pp. 617-619, and *The Gospel of Luke*, pp. 619-620.

27. See J. Fitzmyer, "The Story of the Dishonest Manager (Lk. 16:1-13)," *Theological Studies*, Vol. 25 (1964), p. 27.

28. This is the conclusion of most modern translations. The RSV translates *ho kurios* in vs. 3, 5, 8a as "master" and clearly indicates that *ho kurios* in v. 8a does not refer to Jesus. This is also true of the NEB, NIV, JB, and NASB.

29. So J. D. M. Derrett, "Fresh Light on St. Luke XVI. 1. The Parable of the Unjust Steward," NTS, Vol. 7 (1961), pp. 198-219.

30. So Fitzmyer, "The Story of the Dishonest Manager (Lk. 16:1-13)," pp. 23-42.

31. Jeremias, *The Parables of Jesus*, p. 181.

32. Kenneth Ewing Bailey, *Poet and Peasant: A Literary Cultural Approach to the Parables in Luke* (Wm. B. Eerdmans Publishing Co., 1976), pp. 89-91.

33. Ibid., pp. 95-102.

34. L. John Topel, "On the Injustice of the Unjust Steward: Luke 16:1-13," CBQ, Vol. 37 (1975), p. 218 n. 13.

35. Cf. Manson, *The Sayings of Jesus*, p. 292, who sees the master saying something like: "This is a fraud; but it is a most ingenious fraud. The steward is a rascal; but he is a wonderfully clever rascal."

36. Jeremias, *The Parables of Jesus*, p. 47.

37. Note the *hoti* of v. 8 which gives the ground for the commendation!

38. TDNT, Vol. VII. p. 484. See also Bailey, *Poet and Peasant*, pp. 105-106.

39. Jeremias, *The Parables of Jesus*, p. 182.

40. On the latter, see Topel, "On the Injustice of the Unjust Steward: Luke 16:1-3," p. 221, and above, p. 79.

41. Two additional arguments that have been given for seeing the arrangement of Luke 14:26-33 as being Lukan are found in Peter G. Jarvis, "The Tower-builder and the King Going to War," ET, Vol. 77 (1966), p. 196. Jarvis points out that the parables interrupt the continuity of Luke 14:26-27 and 33 and argues with Jeremias, *The Parables of Jesus*, p. 106, that the parables make a different point (self-testing) than 14:26-27 and 33 (self-sacrifice). The latter argument seems weak, however, in that the parables' emphasis on "counting the cost" is closely related to "self-sacrifice."

42. Jeremias, *The Parables of Jesus*, p. 150.

43. So Linnemann, *Parables of Jesus*, pp. 117 and 181 n. 13, and especially Philip Barton Payne, "The Authenticity of the Parable of the Sower and Its Interpretation," in *Gospel Perspectives*, ed. by France and Wenham, Vol. I, pp. 181-186

CHAPTER 9.
THE GOD OF THE PARABLES

1. Note in Luke 4:18-19 where Jesus ends the Isa 61:1-2 quotation!

2. This is the view of Jack T. Sanders, "Tradition and Redaction in Luke XV.11-32," NTS, Vol. 15 (1968), pp. 433-438.

3. So Linnemann, *Parables of Jesus*, p. 152 n. 20.

4. Sanders, "Tradition and Redaction in Luke XV.11-32," p. 435. Another argument given by Sanders is that there are no truly authentic two-part parables in the Synoptic tradition. The nonauthenticity of the latter part of Luke 16:19-31, however, is far from an established fact.

5. See Joachim Jeremias, "Tradition und Redaktion im Lukas 15," ZNW, Vol. 62 (1971), pp. 172-189; John J. O'Rourke, "Some Notes on Luke XV. 11-32," NTS, Vol. 18 (1971), pp. 431-433; and especially Charles E. Carlston, "Reminiscence and Redaction in Luke 15:11-32," JBL, Vol. 94 (1975), pp. 368-390.

6. Carlston, "Reminiscence and Redaction," p. 383. This, of course, does not mean that Luke did not work the parable to meet his needs and aims.

7. Ibid., pp. 387-388.

8. Note especially Luke 15:29, where the older son states, "Lo, these many years I have served you, and I never disobeyed your command."

9. Cf. Linnemann, *Parables of Jesus*, p. 74, who states, "The parable remains all the time pure narrative which bears its own weight. In no place does it become an allegory in which 'picture part' and 'reality part' are identical."

10. J. Duncan M. Derrett, "Law in the New Testament: The Parable of the Prodigal Son," NTS, Vol. 14 (1967), p. 60 n. 3.

11. So Linnemann, *Parables of Jesus*, pp. 74-75.

12. b. Baba Metzia 19a (Soncino Press, p. 119). See also the discussion in Derrett, "Law in the New Testament: The Parable of the Prodigal Son," pp. 62-63.

13. The imperative "give" should not be interpreted as a demand by the younger son, for he had no grounds for such a demand. The imperative is best understood as an imperative of entreaty or request.

14. See Linnemann, *Parables of Jesus,* p. 60.

15. Bailey, *Poet and Peasant,* pp. 163-164.

16. b. Baba Kamma 82b (Soncino Press, p. 470).

17. The question of why the prodigal remained hungry even though he wanted to fill himself on the carob pods the swine ate has never been satisfactorily answered. Jeremias, *The Parables of Jesus,* p. 129, suggests that the prodigal was too disgusted to eat the carob pods, but this is strange since carob pods are quite edible and in times of starvation one is seldom fussy as to what one will eat. Linnemann, *Parables of Jesus,* p. 151 n. 11, suggests that the owner did not permit the prodigal to satisfy his hunger by eating the carob pods. Against this it must be asked whether it is not strange to work simply to starve! Bailey, *Poet and Peasant,* pp. 171-173, has suggested that the carob pods referred to in the parable are not the edible *Caratonia siliqua* but rather a wild carob pod which is bitter and lacks nourishment. At this time there does not seem to be a truly satisfactory explanation to this question.

18. Jeremias, *New Testament Theology,* pp. 152-153.

19. Derrett, "Law in the New Testament: The Parable of the Prodigal Son," p. 65. Derrett points out that the younger son sinned not so much in his dissipation but because in his dissipation he no longer had the means to take care of his father. This, far more than his association with harlots, would have been seen by Jesus' audience as his great sin.

20. Bailey, *Poet and Peasant,* p. 181, gives a number of Near Eastern examples of how such running would be considered a most humiliating act of behavior. He even gives a recent example of a pastor who was not accepted by a particular church in the Near East because "he walked down the street too fast."

21. Cf. Gen 41:42; Esth 3:10; 8:8; 1 Macc 6:15; Josephus, *Antiquities,* 12. 360.

22. Cf. here also the refusal of the lawyer in Luke 10:37 to acknowledge that the Samaritan was indeed the one who proved to be the neighbor and fulfilled the Law! He states instead, "The one who showed mercy on him."

23. Derrett, "Law in the New Testament: The Parable of the Prodigal Son," p. 67.

24. See Marshall, *The Gospel of Luke,* pp. 598-599.

25. The various attempts to see the elder brother of the parable as also being lost seems to be a pressing of the details. That Pharisees and scribes who held the attitude portrayed in Luke 15:1-2 were lost goes without saying, but the intention of Jesus in the parable is to defend his fellowshiping with publicans and sinners rather than to show the lostness of his critics.

26. Jeremias, *The Parables of Jesus,* p. 131. Cf. also Derrett's fine summary of how Jesus hoped the Pharisees and scribes would respond: "You have agreed that the prodigal son was wicked and that his repentance was justified. You have agreed that the father was entitled to reinstate him as a member of the family. And you are satisfied that this can be done without loss to those to whom by contract the inheritance belongs. Have you not, thereby, admitted that the elder son's argument is wrong (as it obviously was), and therefore that the non-religious, the last-minute-pious, are as much entitled as you are to the

Father's favor? If you still cherish doubts about this, to whom are you to be likened? To Cain, Adonijah, Eliab, elder brothers of Joseph? To the Midianites, and still worse the Edomites?" ("Law in the New Testament: The Parable of the Prodigal Son," pp. 72-73).

27. I. Howard Marshall, *Luke: Historian and Theologian* (Zondervan Publishing House, 1971), p. 92, states, "It is our thesis that the idea of salvation supplies the key to the theology of Luke."

28. *Metanoia:* Luke 3:3, 8; 5:32; 15:7; 24:47; Matt 3:8, 11; Mark 1:4; *metanoeō:* Luke 10:13; 11:32; 13:3, 5; 15:7, 10; 16:30; 17:3-4; Matt 3:2; 4:17, 11:20, 21; 12:41; Mark 1:15; 6:12; *epistrephō:* Luke 1:16-17; 22:32; Matt 13:15; Mark 4:12.

29. See above, pp. 78-79.

30. Carlston, "Reminiscence and Redaction in Luke 15:11-32," pp. 384-385, argues that the parable lacks the particular Lukan emphasis on the moral dimension of repentance. This may be true and it is a point in favor of the traditional origin of the parable, but Luke certainly did not see the parable as standing in conflict with his own view or else he would simply have omitted it. (Actually we should say, "He would not have chosen to include it,"for Luke purposely chose to include this parable in his Gospel.) It may be that the traditional view of repentance found in the parable does not portray certain aspects of repentance that Luke frequently emphasizes, but there was more than sufficient overlapping, so that Luke chose to include it in his Gospel.

31. So J. Duncan M. Derrett, "Workers in the Vineyard: A Parable of Jesus," *JJS,* Vol. 25 (1974), p. 88.

32. So Linnemann, *Parables of Jesus,* pp. 82-83.

33. It is uncertain as to whether one denarius was a generous wage (so Linnemann, *Parables of Jesus,* p. 68) or simply a fair wage (so Derrett, "Workers in the Vineyard," p. 68). The issue is of no major consequence, however, since for the people who worked only one hour it was indeed a generous wage.

34. It should be noted that v. 13b-c combines the agreements made to the first- and third-hour workers (v. 13b "wrong" corresponds with v. 4 "right," and v. 13c "agree . . . for a denarius" corresponds with v. 2 "agreeing . . . for a denarius"). It would therefore appear that no emphasis should be placed on the supposedly different bases for hiring the various workers.

35. Derrett, "Workers in the Vineyard," pp. 73-74, seeks to give a rational rather than a literary explanation for the reversal of the order and concludes that the order is historically reasonable. Matt 20:1-16, however, is not a recounting of a historical event but a parable! The parable furthermore requires this reversal of order or else the first workers would not be present to complain.

36. This fact alone is sufficient to refute such allegorical interpretations as that of Irenaeus (see pp. 43-44, above) and Origen (see p. 45, above).

37. Cf. Günther Bornkamm, *Jesus of Nazareth,* trans. by Irene and Fraser McLuskey (Harper & Brothers, 1960), p. 142, who states, "The idea of the merit of good works and man's claim upon God is most clearly shaken and abolished in the parable of the laborers in the vineyard (Mt xx. 1-16)."

38. Since I have said that the parable does not teach the doctrine of "justification by faith," it nevertheless must be observed that it does teach the graciousness and mercy of God which is one of the essential foundations upon which the doctrine of justification by faith is built.

39. So Jeremias, *The Parables of Jesus,* p. 37.

40. Ibid., p. 38.

41. So, for instance, ibid., pp. 34-38, 110-111. On purely textual grounds the clause "for many be called, but few chosen" found in the King James Version has been omitted in the modern translations because of its being a later scribal addition.

42. This is, of course, not the only possible reason why Matthew may have placed this parable after the account of the rich young ruler. It may be that he saw a similarity in the message of these two accounts as well.

43. So Jeremias, *The Parables of Jesus*, p. 37; C. L. Mitton, "The Workers in the Vineyard (Matthew 20:1-16)," ET, Vol. 77 (1966), p. 308.

44. If this is true, then it may be that the entire question of the parable's integrity and authenticity should be reconsidered since one of the main arguments against the proverb's authenticity, i.e., that it conflicts with the meaning of the parable, is no longer valid. In fact it would appear that the proverb may fit very well the *Sitz im Leben* in which the parable was uttered by Jesus.

45. The conclusion that the woman of Luke 7:36-50 was probably a sinner in this sense is due to 7:47-50.

46. Francis Thompson's poem, "The Hound of Heaven," captures well this aspect of God's character.

47. Note here that Paul was criticized over his too-good-to-be-true gospel of grace! See Rom 3:5; 6:1, 14.

Chapter 10.
The Final Judgment

1. I have borrowed this term from Manson, *The Sayings of Jesus*, p. 249.

2. See Jeremias, *The Parables of Jesus*, Index, and pp. 206-210; Archibald M. Hunter, *Interpreting the Parables* (Westminster Press, 1961), pp. 88-90, 122. Cf. also Manson, *The Teaching of Jesus*, who on p. 37 refers to Matt 25:31-46 as a parable but excludes it from his list of parables on pp. 66-68.

3. Enoch 46:4f.; 62:6f. The dating of Enoch 37-71 is much debated. It is most unlikely, however, that the author of Enoch 37-71, whoever he may be and whenever he wrote, obtained his portrait of the Son of man as judge from Matthew's Gospel!

4. David R. Catchpole, "The Poor on Earth and the Son of Man in Heaven. A Re-appraisal of Matthew xxv. 31-46," BJRL, Vol. 61 (1978), p. 384.

5. See ibid., pp. 383-387, for a strong argument in favor of the authenticity of this portrayal in Matt 25:31-46.

6. Lamar Cope, "Matthew xxv. 31-46—'The Sheep and the Goats' Reinterpreted," NT, Vol. 11 (1969), p. 34, points out that "Matthew uses a closing reference to future judgment as a technique for concluding the discourses of Jesus, and he does so in ways which often show his own style and vocabulary. (See Matt 7:21-27; 10:40-42; 13:49-50; 18:35; 25:31-46. Cf. also Matt 3:12.)"

7. So Cope, "Matthew xxv. 31-46," pp. 41-43, who argues that Matthew created this passage. See also Bultmann, *The History of the Synoptic Tradition*, p. 124.

8. Hunter, *Interpreting the Parables*, p. 118. For a similar view, see Jeremias, *The Parables of Jesus*, pp. 208-209; J. A. T. Robinson, "The 'Parable' of the Sheep and the Goats," NTS, Vol. 2 (1955), pp. 225, 236; Manson, *The Teaching of Jesus*, p. 249; Catchpole, "The Poor on Earth," pp. 383-397; and H. E. W. Turner, "The Parable of the Sheep and the Goats (Matthew 25:31-46)," ET, Vol. 77 (1966), pp. 243-246.

9. So Turner, "The Parable of the Sheep and the Goats," p. 243.

10. See Amos 3:14; 5:18; Zeph 1:7f.; Joel 3:11f.; etc. For a discussion of this theme in the Old Testament see Gerhard von Rad, *Old Testament Theology*, trans. by D. M. G. Stalker (Harper & Row, 1965), Vol. II, pp. 119-125; and in the apocalyptic literature, see D. S. Russell, *The Method and Message of Jewish Apocalyptic* (The Old Testament Library) (Westminster Press, 1964), pp. 94-96, 379-385.

11. See Catchpole, "The Poor on Earth," pp. 387-389, for a discussion of this expression in Matthew.

12. See TDNT, Vol. 2, pp. 37-40.

13. What we mean here, of course, is that Jesus' listeners understood this concept, so that Jesus did not have to explain this to them.

14. See b. Kiddushin 41b (Soncino Press, p. 206); 43a (Soncino Press, p. 216); TDNT, Vol. 1, p. 45.

15. Cf. here also John 13:20 and 2 Clement 17:5.

16. Note how Paul discovered this on the road to Damascus when he in his persecution of the brethren, i.e., the church, heard from the risen Christ, "Saul, Saul, why do you persecute *me?*" (Acts 9:4, italics added).

17. Note here how Luther had a similar emphasis due in part to his countering a similar error!

18. See above, pp. 137-140.

19. By faith we do not here mean simply *fides informis*, i.e., an intellectual assent to the truth of certain propositions, but rather *fiducia*, i.e., a committed entrusting of oneself to the God of grace who offers to all forgiveness on the basis of grace through faith.

20. Jeremias, *The Parables of Jesus*, p. 207.

21. See TDNT, Vol. 1, pp. 145-146.

22. Cf. also Matt 23:8.

23. J. Ramsay Michaels, "Apostolic Hardship and Righteous Gentiles—A Study of Matthew 25:31-46," JBL, Vol. 84 (1965), pp. 27-37, in this regard draws an interesting parallel between the afflictions that Paul mentions as having endured as an apostle in 2 Cor 11:23-29 and the six acts of love mentioned in our passage.

24. Jeremias, *The Parables of Jesus*, p. 207.

25. In this regard see the important article by Heinz Schürmann, "Die vorösterlichen Anfänge der Logientradition. Versuch eines formgeschichtlichen Zugangs zum Leben Jesu," in *Der historische Jesus und der kerygmatische Christus*, ed. by Helmut Ristow and Karl Matthiae (Berlin: Evangelische Verlagsanstalt, 1961), pp. 342-370.

26. So Jeremias, *The Parables of Jesus*, p. 225.

27. John A. McEvoy, "Realized Eschatology and the Kingdom Parables,"

CBQ, Vol. 9 (1947), p. 343, points out that such a net was about 400 to 500 meters long and three meters wide.

28. Hunter, *Interpeting the Parables,* p. 50 n. 1, states, "We judge that Jesus did not need to interpret his parables." For some of the more recent scholars, the autonomous, polyvalent nature of the parables requires that Jesus did not interpret his parables since then they would no longer be "open-ended."

29. See Raymond E. Brown, "Parable and Allegory Reconsidered," in his *New Testament Essays* (Doubleday & Co., 1968), pp. 321-333.

30. See Payne, "The Authenticity of the Parable of the Sower and Its Interpretation," in *Gospel Perspectives,* ed. by France and Wenham, Vol. I, pp. 17-172.

31. So Kingsbury, *The Parables of Jesus in Matthew 13,* pp. 118-123. Kingsbury's interpretation of this parable seems at times, to this writer at least, a bit too allegorical even for the third *Sitz im Leben.*

32. Jeremias, *The Parables of Jesus,* p. 85.

33. Hebrews 9:26 is the only other passage in which we find "close" *(sunteleia)* but the expression here is "close of the ages."

34. So Jeremias, *The Parables of Jesus,* p. 85.

35. Ibid., pp. 84-85. Jeremias' discussion of this passage begins on p. 81.

36. So Crossan, "The Seed Parables of Jesus," JBL, Vol. 92 (1973), pp. 260-261, who argues that the conflict in vs. 37-39 (the field is the "world") and vs. 41-43 (the field is the "kingdom," i.e., the church) is due to Matthew's conflict in his interpretation of the field as the church with that of the pre-Matthean tradition which interpreted the field as the world.

37. So Kingsbury, *The Parables of Jesus in Matthew 13,* p. 65.

38. So David R. Catchpole, "John the Baptist, Jesus and the Parable of the Tares," SJT, Vol. 31 (1978), p. 369.

39. So Jeremias, *The Parables of Jesus,* pp. 224-225.

40. The Gospel of Thomas like Matthew speaks of an enemy coming at night and sowing the weeds. It would appear therefore that Catchpole's elimination of this aspect of the parable seems indefensible.

41. So Boucher, *The Mysterious Parable,* pp. 39-40.

42. Contra Kinsgbury, *The Parables of Jesus in Matthew 13,* pp. 117-118.

43. Gospel of Thomas 57 from *Synopsis Quattuor Evangeliorum* (Stuttgart: Deutsche Bibelstiftung, 1978), with the Greek words omitted.

44. Jeremias, *The Parables of Jesus,* p. 85.

45. So Hunter, *Interpreting the Parables,* p. 46.

46. Here is a detail that not only invites allegorization but may demand it.

47. See, however, Brown, "Parable and Allegory Reconsidered," p. 326, for the view that the essence of this interpretation goes back to Jesus.

48. Kingsbury, *The Parables of Jesus in Matthew 13,* p. 66, seeks to argue that the interpretation of the parable is "only apparently, not really, an explanation of the parable of the Tares." He is surely incorrect in this, however, and because of this his view that the parable (not the interpretation) signifies for Matthew that "the Church is not now to pronounce judgment on unbelieving Israel by evoking a formal withdrawal from it" (p. 75) is not convincing. Such an interpretation of the Evangelist's understanding of the parable can only exist if Matthew did not compose or think that the interpretation of the parable in 13:36-43 was in fact the interpretation of the parable! Yet surely Matt 13:36

must mean that for Matthew what follows is in fact the interpretation of the parable of the tares.

49. The present writer realizes that in some theological circles the term "harmonize" has negative connotations, but he believes that common courtesy should always attempt to seek consistency in the writings or teachings of any reasonably intelligent person. At times this may not be possible, for reasonably intelligent people are at times inconsistent, but one should always in politeness assume consistency unless proven otherwise.

50. George Eldon Ladd, *Jesus and the Kingdom* (Harper & Row, 1964), p. 230.

51. See ibid., p. 229.

52. See Catchpole, "John the Baptist," pp. 569-570.

INDEX OF REFERENCES

Ancient Authors

INDEX OF AUTHORS AND SUBJECTS